Pat Sloan's
Teach Me to Machine Quilt

Learn the basics of walking-foot & free-motion quilting

Happy Quilting
Lina

Martingale®
Create with Confidence

Pat Sloan's Teach Me to Machine Quilt:
Learn the Basics of Walking-Foot & Free-Motion Quilting
© 2016 by Pat Sloan

Martingale®
19021 120th Ave. NE, Ste. 102
Bothell, WA 98011-9511 USA
ShopMartingale.com

Printed in China
21 20 19 18 17   8 7 6 5 4 3 2

Library of Congress Cataloging-in-Publication Data
is available upon request.

ISBN: 978-1-60468-831-3

MISSION STATEMENT

We empower makers who use fabric and yarn
to make life more enjoyable.

CREDITS

PUBLISHER AND
CHIEF VISIONARY OFFICER
Jennifer Erbe Keltner

CONTENT DIRECTOR
Karen Costello Soltys

DESIGN MANAGER
Adrienne Smitke

MANAGING EDITOR
Tina Cook

COVER AND
INTERIOR DESIGNER
Regina Girard

ACQUISITIONS EDITOR
Karen M. Burns

PHOTOGRAPHER
Brent Kane

TECHNICAL EDITOR
Nancy Mahoney

ILLUSTRATOR
Lisa Lauch

COPY EDITOR
Durby Peterson

*Many thanks to Lynn Austin of Kirkland, Washington,
for allowing Martingale to photograph the
quilts for this book in her home.*

Contents

 See online videos

Bonus Online Technique Videos! When you see this icon in the book, visit ShopMartingale.com/PatSloanVideos to view my special bonus techniques!

Come Stitch with Me

From the first bedspread I made to the latest baby quilt for my great-nephew, I wanted to quilt my own quilts. When I made that bedspread "quilt" many years ago and tied it with yarn, it never occurred to me to have someone else quilt it. When I took my first official quilting class, where all the techniques were done by hand, we hand quilted our own quilts.

I loved learning all the steps in the quiltmaking process and then doing each of them myself. After awhile I was machine quilting with my walking foot—doing fun and easy things to give my quilts another layer of design. Eventually, I wanted to stitch swirls and quilt faster, so I learned free-motion quilting too.

Each type of machine quilting—walking foot and free motion—takes practice. You need to invest time to increase your skills. But some types of machine quilting can be mastered faster than others, so don't hesitate to get started.

Part of the fun of being a quiltmaker is completing and using your treasured quilt. Maybe you give the quilt away, maybe you keep it. Either way, when we do all the steps ourselves, it is so rewarding.

On the following pages, I'll teach you how easy it is to quilt your own project using two methods, "Machine Quilting with a Walking Foot" (page 17) and "Free-Motion Machine Quilting" (page 32). Both methods give you a set of skills to use right now on your stack of projects that need to be quilted. Once you're comfortable with these techniques, you may want to move on to other methods, or maybe you'll continue using these skills and spend time creating more quilt tops! Either way, you'll have finished the quilt yourself.

Often quilters tell me they don't want to practice. They ask me if there's a way to practice on "real" projects. I totally understand that! We don't have a lot of extra time, and many of us are just impatient. (I'm raising my hand to that one!) I have some easy solutions, and I'll show you a few ways to practice while making a finished item.

The power of learning a basic set of go-to techniques is that you can use them for years to come to finish your quilts. But you'll also have the freedom to grow beyond that. In these pages I'll share a whole set of smaller quilts to make and practice on. I'll also show you a table runner quilted several different ways so you can compare the looks. After trying the techniques, you'll develop a set of go-to quilting designs that you can make your own for future quiltmaking.

Because we all want to finish our quilts, quilting them ourselves is a sweet ending to the project. Now, let's go sew!

Yes, You Can
Machine Quilt!

Even if you've never quilted a quilt by machine, I know you can do it. Why? Because I'm here to help you. In the pages that follow, you'll find everything you need to get started—from setting up your machine (stitch length, the right needle, the right type of thread, and so on) to basting your quilt top to taking your first stitches. If you're brand new to machine quilting, start there.

Then move on to "Machine Quilting with a Walking Foot" on page 17. A walking foot is a presser foot that moves both the top and bottom layers of fabric evenly through the machine, so the movement will be familiar, like when you're sewing patchwork.

When you're ready to move beyond straight-line designs, head to "Free-Motion Machine Quilting" on page 32. Here you'll learn about moving the quilt yourself, rather than having the machine feeding the quilt for you. This technique gives you the freedom to create just about any design you'd like. I'll help you get started, show you some of my favorite design motifs, and share my ideas for building your skills. This technique will take a bit more practice, since you'll be in charge of moving the fabric where you want it to go. But with time you'll be able to quilt loops and swirls, echos and curves—whatever you can imagine!

Getting Ready to Machine Quilt

Preparing your quilt properly is the groundwork for successful quilting. Whether you plan to use a walking foot or want to free-motion quilt your project, now's the time to clean up the quilt top and make sure it's square, choose a batting, and prepare the backing. You also need to adequately baste your quilt to avoid a whole host of problems while quilting it.

Preparing the Quilt Top

Having a neat and tidy quilt top is key to successfully finishing the quilt. Here are my four easy steps.

1. **Check for popped seams.** Place the quilt top right side up and scan it for any seams that might not have been sewn properly. It's much easier to fix any errors now rather than after the quilt is basted.

2. **Trim loose threads on the right and wrong sides of the quilt top.** I trim threads as I go, but I still find stray threads. Often, long dark threads are visible through the top. Look for any seams that may be twisted and re-press, if needed.

3. **Square up the quilt top.** If the quilt top isn't square, it won't get better after basting. (By "square," I mean that the edges are parallel to one another and the corners are each a true 90°. This goes for rectangular quilts too!) Measure the width of the quilt top across the top, middle, and bottom edges. The measurements should all be the same. Measure the length of the quilt top in the same way. Place a large square ruler in each corner to make sure the corners are square. If the border is wavy, that means the border strips weren't measured correctly before sewing them to the quilt. To remedy this, remove the border. Measure the quilt top and border strips again, trim the strips as needed, and then sew the border to the quilt top.

4. **Stay stitch around the quilt.** Sew about ⅛" from each edge **(photo 1).** The stitching will stabilize the seams. This is especially important when there's patchwork on the outer edge of the quilt top. You don't want the seams to come undone during the basting and quilting process.

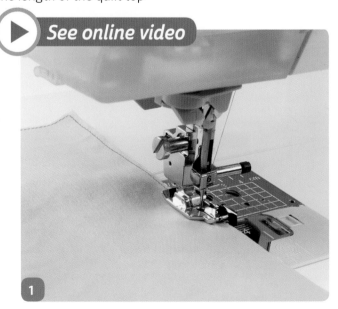

See online video

See Pat demonstrate stay stitching at ShopMartingale.com/PatSloanVideos

Making the Quilt Backing

Starting with my first quilt, I made the backing using leftover fabrics from the quilt top. If I didn't have leftover fabrics, I sometimes used fabrics that fell into the "I don't know why I bought them" category, so I could use them up! I still piece a lot of my quilt backs, but now I prefer to have the backing complement the front, particularly for larger quilts where the backing will be seen.

For large quilts, the backing should be at least 8" wider than the top, which allows 4" of backing on all sides so you can position the batting and top accurately. For smaller quilts, such as wall hangings and table runners, make the backing 4" to 5" wider than the top, which allows at least 2" on all sides.

Most fabric is about 40" wide, once you account for shrinkage and removing the selvages. Quilts less than 35" wide can use one length of fabric for the backing. If the quilt is more than 36" wide, you'll need to piece the backing. Or, for larger quilts, you can purchase a "wide quilt back," which measures 90" or 108" wide.

Backing Yardage Chart

Quilt Size	Dimensions	Backing	2¼"-Wide Binding
Twin	63" x 87"	5 yards	⅝ yard
Double	78" x 87"	5 yards	¾ yard
Queen	84" x 92"	7½ yards	¾ yard
King	100" x 92"	8¼ yards	⅞ yard

Calculating Backing Fabric

Determining how much fabric you need for a backing sounds scary, but it's actually quite simple. Here's my formula.

1. Add the extra inches needed for a quilting allowance (4" to 8") to both the width and length measurements of the quilt top. For instance, if the quilt is 60" x 80", the backing fabric needs to be at least 68" x 88".

2. Divide the width of the quilt by the width of the backing fabric. Round up the result to the nearest whole number. In this instance, the calculation would be as follows: 68" ÷ 40" = 1.7; round up to 2. The result is how many lengths of fabric you need.

3. Multiply the length of the quilt by the number of fabric lengths you need. Divide the result by 36", and that equals the number of yards you need to buy. The calculation would be as follows: 88" x 2 lengths = 176". 176" ÷ 36" = 4.88 yards. So, you'll need 5 yards to back a 60" x 80" quilt.

Pieced Backing Options

If you're using just one fabric for the backing (as opposed to piecing a scrappy backing), you'll need to calculate how much backing fabric is necessary based on the width of the quilt top. For quilts that are 40" to 60" wide, use two or three lengths of fabric with either one or two *horizontal* seams as shown **(fig. 1).** Be sure to remove the selvage and join the lengths of fabric using a ¼" seam allowance.

For quilts that are 60" wide or larger, use two or three lengths of fabric with either one or two *vertical* seams as shown **(fig. 2).**

It's fun using leftover fabric from the quilt top to make a scrappy pieced backing. I might have a wide section, then a strip of either scraps or single fabric, and then the same fabric again on the other side of the strip. Or I might use the center for randomly sized pieces of leftover fabrics and then add wide strips to both sides of the patchwork center **(fig. 3).**

All great achievements require time.

— DAVID J. SCHWARTZ —

Fig. 1

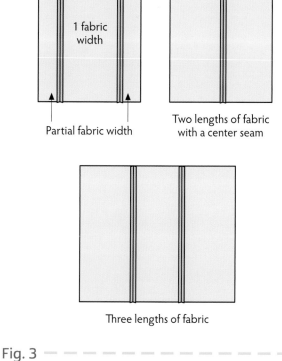

Three lengths of fabric

Two lengths of fabric with a center seam

Fig. 2

1 fabric width

Partial fabric width

Two lengths of fabric with a center seam

Three lengths of fabric

Fig. 3

Cut the backing lengthwise into 2 different-width pieces and add pieced strips in the center.

Batting

Batting **(photo 1)** is available in many different styles—from the fiber content to the thickness (or loft). I've always preferred a flat (or low-loft) batting that doesn't require super close quilting. Every batting tells you on the package how closely it should be quilted.

I like either 100% cotton batting or a batting with a higher percentage of cotton, such as 80% cotton/20% polyester or 60% cotton/40% polyester. These battings are thinner and crinkle more when washed. For a little more loft, I like 100% wool batting. The extra loft means it's not as easy for a beginner to use because the quilt sandwich will be thicker. So I recommend starting with a cotton or cotton/ polyester batting. Keep in mind, some 100% cotton battings need to be quilted more closely than others, so check the label or packaging for details.

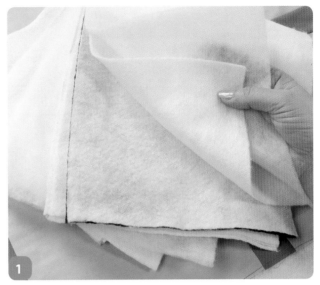

Batting Sampler

A batting sampler is a great reference. I recommend making 7" x 10" samples and keeping them in plastic sleeves in a three-ring binder. There are two types of samples to keep so that you not only know what's available, but also what you like stitching on and what you don't.

- **Different types of batting, unquilted.** Go in with several people to buy packages of different brands and types of batting. Cut each batting into 7" x 10" pieces and divvy up the pieces among the people in your group. If you're attending a large quilt show, look for batting manufacturers and pick up their batting sample cards.

- **Quilted samples.** Using a light-colored solid that you can write on, make a quilt sandwich. Next, stitch on the quilt sandwich. Last, on the stitched sample, write the fiber content and brand of batting, as well as other information about the batting from the label (such as how closely it needs to be quilted), or staple the batting label to the sample.

Basting

I prepare my quilts using one of two methods: pin basting or spray basting. Which method I use depends on the size of the quilt. I like to baste, but I'm pretty sure this is most quilters' least favorite part of the process. Good basting will seriously improve the look of your finished quilting and make the quilting easier to do. So take the time to do it right.

PIN BASTING

If you're going to use only one basting method, this is the one to learn. I find that pin basting is the easiest way to baste a quilt sandwich. I pin baste all my larger quilts. For this method, you'll need the following.

- Lots of 1" safety pins

- Clamps

- Clean, flat surface to tape the back to, such as a large table or uncarpeted floor

- Kwik Klip to close the pins. This tool is optional, but I've found that it saves time and my hands. (See photo 4 on page 13.)

1. **Lay the freshly pressed backing** wrong side up on a clean, flat surface. Smooth out all the wrinkles. Clamp the edges to the table about every 6" to 8", gently pulling the backing taut before clamping it in place **(photo 1).** The object is to make sure the backing is smooth, flat, and wrinkle free, but not stretched out of shape.

See online video

See Pat demonstrate pin basting at ShopMartingale.com/PatSloanVideos

Basting Option

If you don't have a table, place the backing wrong side up on a clean floor. Use masking tape or painter's tape to tape the edges to the floor.

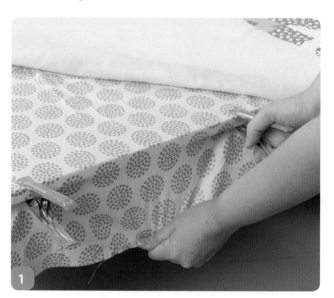

2. **Center the batting** on top of the backing, patting it smooth and making sure the edges are parallel. Being careful not to tug and twist, just gently lift the batting up and let it float down to get

it straight on the back **(photo 2).** If you're using a packaged batting that's been folded, take it out of the package the day before and fluff it out to let the creases relax before you start to baste.

3. **Center the pressed quilt top,** right side up, on the backing and batting. Check to be certain that both the backing and batting extend several inches past the quilt top on all sides. Smooth out any wrinkles, working from the center to the outer edges, again taking care not to stretch any part of the quilt out of shape **(photo 3).**

4. **Starting in the center,** place pins every 4", or even closer **(photo 4).** Place the pins in rows, working your way to the outer edges. Don't remove the clamps until the entire quilt is covered edge to edge with pins.

5. **Pin or machine baste** around the outer edges. Trim the batting, leaving 1" on all sides of the quilt top. When sewing, remove each pin before you come to it.

Safety Pins

Not all safety pins are created equal! Test any new package of pins before adding them to your current ones. Sometimes a batch of pins will have a problem, such as points that are not sharp enough for fabric, or shafts that have burrs. You don't want to dump a bad batch in with your good pins. Ask me how I know this! To test, insert a few of the pins through a quilt to make sure they work smoothly.

Often I find that dry cleaners have the best quality pins. See if you can buy a set of pins from your dry cleaner.

I store my pins in an unusual manner, but it saves time. When I remove the pins as I'm quilting, I just pop them into a jar, leaving them open. That way, the pins are open when I'm ready to use them. And, it reduces the number of times I need to open and close the pins.

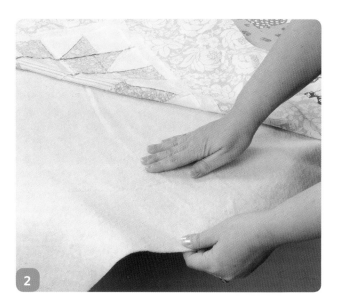

SPRAY BASTING

I like to use spray basting for smaller projects. It's quicker and easier than pin basting, but frankly not as easy for me to manage on a large quilt because I like to have the backing flat. Be sure to follow the manufacturer's instructions for the product you're using. Make sure to work in a well-ventilated area.

1. Lay the freshly pressed backing wrong side up on a clean, flat surface. Smooth out all the wrinkles. Anchor the backing with clamps, being careful not to stretch it out of shape.

2. Center the batting on top of the backing, patting it smooth and making sure the edges are parallel. Fold the batting back about halfway and spray the backing evenly with basting spray. Unfold the batting on the backing fabric and gently smooth in place, starting in the center and working outward. Repeat for the other half of the batting and backing.

3. Center the pressed quilt top, right side up, on the batting and backing. Fold the quilt top back about halfway. Spray the batting evenly with basting spray **(photo 1)**. Unfold the quilt top and gently smooth in place, starting in the center and working outward. Repeat for the other half of the quilt top.

4. Remove the clamps. Machine baste around the outer edges and trim the batting, leaving 1" on all sides of the quilt top. You may want to press both sides of the quilt sandwich. Pressing helps dry the adhesive and makes the quilt sandwich flat.

Spray-Basting Cautions

Beware of overspray; it can leave a sticky residue. To avoid this, lay a large bedsheet on the surface first for protection. When you're done basting, it's easy to pop the sheet into the laundry to remove the basting spray.

Be sure to wipe away any overspray. Or better yet, take the table outside to baste when you can!

Thread

My thread of choice is Aurifil 100% cotton, because it's low-lint and works beautifully in all my quilts. For all brands of thread, the higher the number, the thinner the thread. Below are a few of the thread weights available.

- **50 weight** is a standard thread for sewing **(photo 1).** It works great for both walking-foot and free-motion quilting. I recommend using the same thread in the bobbin and in the needle.

- **40 weight** is slightly heavier than 50 weight **(photo 2).** Use it when you want the quilting to be a bit more visible. This thread can be used for both walking-foot and free-motion quilting. Again, use the same thread in the bobbin and the needle.

- **28 weight** is noticeably thicker than 40 or 50 weight **(photo 3).** This thread is really noticeable and can be used with both walking-foot and free-motion quilting. Try using the same thread in the bobbin; if you're having problems with tension, switch to a 40-weight bobbin thread and test the tension. Adjust it if necessary.

- **12 weight** is the thickest I use for quilting and is suitable only for walking-foot quilting **(photo 4).** Try using a 28-weight thread in the bobbin. If you're having problems with tension, switch to a 40-weight bobbin thread and test the tension.

The best way to know what the thread will look like is to stitch a sample. Gather all the different types of thread you own and stitch a sample of each thread on a three-layer quilt sandwich of backing, batting, and top fabric. Write the weight and brand of each thread on the sample for future reference.

50-weight thread

1

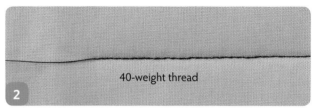

40-weight thread

2

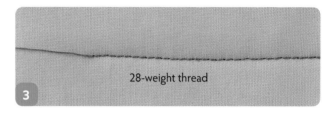

28-weight thread

3

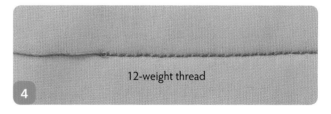

12-weight thread

4

Cone versus Spool

Most threads can be purchased on a cone. A cone needs to be stabilized so that the thread feeds off the cone properly. Your machine may have come with a thread stand, or you can purchase one that sits next to the machine. In a pinch, put the thread cone in a large, plastic cup and feed the thread through the lid!

Before quilting a project, decide the weight and color of thread you want to use. Here are some tips for choosing a thread color based on the quilting design and fabrics in the quilt.

- **Allover quilting design.** If you plan to stitch an allover quilting design, pick several medium-color threads and lay them across the quilt top. Choose a thread that blends nicely with both the light and dark fabrics.

- **Fabrics in warm shades.** If your quilt is predominantly warm colors, such as reds and tans, lay a selection of brown to tan threads across the quilt top. Choose a thread that blends with the fabrics.

- **Fabrics in cool shades.** Conversely, for cool fabrics such as blues and greens, lay a selection of light- to dark-gray threads across the quilt top. Choose a thread that blends with the fabrics **(photo 5).**

- **Change thread colors.** If you aren't quilting an allover design, I suggest using a light thread in the light-patchwork areas and a dark thread in the dark-patchwork areas. Or, you might consider using a medium-color thread in the center of the quilt top and a matching-color thread in the border. Play around with thread colors to achieve the look you want.

5

Make a Sample

If you're not sure how a certain thread color will look, make a small quilt sandwich using the fabrics in the quilt and stitch a bit. Many shades of thread will blend more than you think. Keep in mind that the thread will not be as visible on busier fabrics, such as multicolored florals, as it will be on solids.

Machine Quilting with a Walking Foot

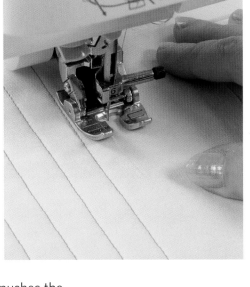

Most sewing machines come with an even-feed presser foot called a walking foot. Some machines even have a built-in even-feed system. A walking foot helps evenly feed the thick quilt sandwich through your machine so you don't create puckers and pleats as you quilt the top, batting, and backing layers together.

I started out quilting my quilts with a walking foot and still use it. I love the effects I get from straight lines as well as decorative stitches. (Yep, you can use some decorative stitches in conjunction with your walking foot to add texture and interest to your quilt.) If you've tried to quilt using a regular presser foot, you've noticed that the top fabric bunches and pulls. A walking foot pushes the top fabric evenly along while the feed dogs underneath control the movement of the backing fabric. The result is that you can quilt beautifully.

From quilting straight lines to decorative stitches, your walking foot offers lots of options. In this section we'll cover setting up your machine, starting and stopping stitching, and what to do when you run out of bobbin thread in the middle of a line of quilting. (It happens to the best of us!)

Setting Up Your Machine

Are you excited and ready to start quilting? First, take two minutes to prep your machine for a successful quilting session.

- **Clean out the lint.** Lift the throat plate (if you can) and use a paintbrush, an awl, a pin, or the tip of a seam ripper to coax any lint buildup out of the way. Batting can make a lot of lint, so be sure to do this regularly for smooth stitching.

- **Put in a new needle.** I use a regular piecing needle, size 70 or 80. But if you find that your thread is breaking, try a size 90 needle, which has a larger eye. Keep in mind that with needles, the higher the number, the larger the needle.

When to Change the Needle

Start listening to the sound the needle makes as you quilt. Listen to a new needle and then listen to one that's been well used. When you hear the needle thump or thunk or punch through the fabric, it's time to change the needle!

I buy a box of 100 needles. Not only do I save money but I can freely change the needle without being concerned about running out.

- **Set the stitch length.** Don't just go with the preset stitch length. That length is good for regular sewing, but when you're stitching through lots of layers, a longer stitch length will work better. I use about 10 to 12 stitches per inch for walking-foot quilting, depending on the thickness of my batting **(photo 1).** The thicker the batting, the longer the stitch length needs to be. Use your test sandwich to see which stitch length works best for you.

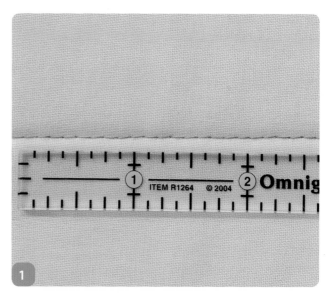

- **Attach the walking foot (photo 2).** If you have a built-in even-feed system, make sure it's engaged.

- **Adjust your chair height.** Be sure you're sitting at the machine with your elbows at a right angle when your hands are on your quilt **(photo 3).** If your machine is too high, your shoulders and arms will ache over time.

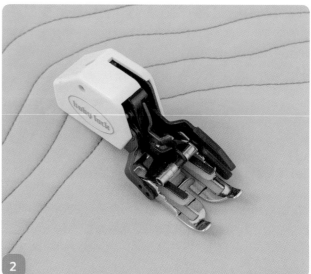

> You never fail until you stop trying.
> — ALBERT EINSTEIN —

Starting to Stitch

Pull the bobbin thread to the surface by putting your needle down into the quilt sandwich and then bringing it back up again. Grab the bobbin thread and pull it to the top **(photo 1).** Hold onto the top and bobbin threads, positioning them to the back of the walking foot. This keeps the threads from creating a mess on the back when you start running the machine. Then you can either use a locking stitch or tie off the threads.

Locking stitch. If your machine has a locking stitch, select this option to take several stitches in place to lock the threads **(photo 2).**

If your machine doesn't have a locking stitch, set the stitch length to 0 and sew several stitches in place. After stitching forward a bit, you can cut the starting threads at the surface of the quilt. Careful! Don't cut the fabric.

Tying off threads. An alternate method is to tie the top and bobbin threads in a knot and bury them in the batting layer of your quilt using a hand-sewing needle **(photo 3).** This takes more time, but you might like it for quilts that will be heavily washed and used.

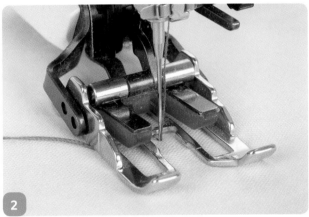

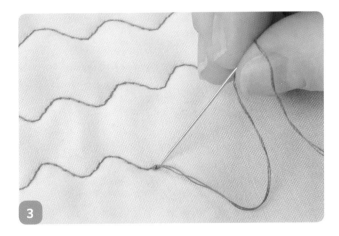

Where Do I Start Stitching?

This is a question that many beginners as well as more seasoned quilters ask me!

- **When stitching an overall design,** I start at the outer edge of the quilt—off the edge of the quilt top but in the batting—and then quilt toward myself.

- **When working inside a block,** I decide what I'm going to quilt and then look for a place where I can take a few stitches before I need to turn or adjust the quilt. It generally works well to start in the middle, along one side of a shape.

Where Do I Stop Stitching?

Stopping works pretty much the same as starting.

- **Use a locking stitch** or set the stitch length to 0 and take a few stitches in place.

- **After quilting for an inch or so,** cut off the threads at the surface of the quilt. Or, knot the threads together and bury them in the batting layer using a hand-sewing needle.

Running Out of Bobbin Thread

Some machines have a sensor that tells you when the bobbin is almost empty. If yours does, listen to it and stop where it's convenient in your design. That makes it easy to pop in a fresh bobbin and restart at an inconspicuous part of your quilt.

If your machine doesn't have a sensor and you're merrily quilting along and then realize you're out of bobbin thread in the middle of your design, here's what to do: Tie off the threads by pulling the top thread to the back of the quilt. Knot the threads together, thread both tails onto a self-threading needle, and weave the tails into the batting under the surface. (If the bobbin thread isn't long enough to thread into a needle, you may need to unpick a few stitches.) Start stitching again where you left off, using your preferred starting method.

Self-Threading Needles

Because they have a slot that guides the thread into the eye of the needle, self-threading needles are super easy to thread, making quick work of burying thread tails.

Life is not made up of minutes, hours, days, weeks, months, or years, but of moments. You must experience each one before you can appreciate it.

— SARAH BAN BREATHNACH —

Let's Get Quilting

Machine quilting a quilt top that you've spent hours piecing or appliquéing can be a bit intimidating. I know, I've been there. You don't want to ruin all your efforts. So before you take your first stitch on an actual quilt top, let's start by making practice quilt sandwiches and learning how to layer, baste, mark (only if you want to!), and quilt them. Then you'll have experience in quilting, maybe unquilting or fixing goofs, and be ready to move on to a real quilt!

Test Sandwiches

Yum, test sandwiches sound good to me! But actually the test sandwiches I'm talking about are mini quilts, about 18" x 20", with backing fabric, batting, and a top fabric.

These practice pieces will help you get the hang of quilting—testing which type of needles, threads, and batting you like; getting your machine's tension set up correctly; and practicing moving and turning your quilt as you go. Make a bunch of test sandwiches and you can try out all the quilting exercises in this book. I use *Bella Solids by Moda Fabrics* for my test sandwiches so I can see the stitches and make notes right on each sample with a marker. If you use a print, it's much harder to see what's going on, and you can't write notes right on the samples. And, what better place to take notes than right on the sample itself, so you can refer back to it and know exactly what you've done.

I keep a stack of quilt sandwiches to use for warming up or trying new designs. I write on the sample the stitch type, stitch length, thread used, and any other settings. Keep your samples in a binder or cute box by your sewing machine. They will be your reference guides.

SIMPLE AND EASY STRAIGHT-LINE QUILTING

Straight-line stitching is a great way to start quilting your own projects. It's not a new technique. Sewing layers of cloth together with straight lines has been done for centuries. You can see it in Japanese boro pieces, kantha quilts from India, and antique quilts our great grandmothers made. Quilting straight lines across a quilt is a soothing process that adds an effective design element. Plus, straight-line quilting gets the job done, which is to hold all the layers together so the quilt can be used! This method can be simple, it can be elegant, and even very detailed. You can do straight stitching in several ways.

- **Edge to edge.** Quilt a series of straight lines across the quilt. Stitch the lines as close together or as far apart as you like, but check your batting requirements: most will call for stitching no more than 4" apart. Use the width of your walking foot as a guide **(photo 1)** or use blue painter's tape in different widths to quickly and easily mark straight lines. Simply stitch next to the tape and pull it off when the row is complete!

Marking Your Quilt

I rarely mark my quilts, but occasionally I need to mark straight lines. Then I use either quilter's tape or painter's tape because they don't leave a sticky residue or any marks on the fabric. If you need to mark your quilt for some other reason, such as to create a grid, I suggest using a sliver of soap or a chalk pencil on dark fabrics. A water-soluble or air-soluble pen works well on light fabrics. Always follow the manufacturer's instructions for the product you're using.

Test the pen or marker on a piece of scrap fabric before using it on your quilt.

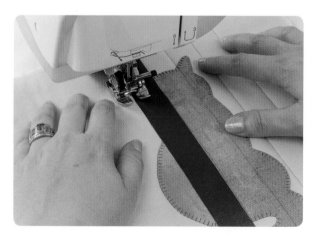

- **Matchstick quilting.** This is the same as edge-to-edge quilting, except the quilting lines are very close together **(photo 2).** It takes longer to do because you're stitching more rows of quilting, but the look is very interesting. For an easy guide, stitch rows the width of your walking foot; then go back and stitch a line down the middle between two stitched lines. Or, stitch two or three lines between the first two lines for a really tight look.

- **Follow block lines.** I prefer to follow a block's lines, quilting about ¼" from the seam **(photo 3).** I don't stitch directly "in the ditch," because I feel that hidden stitching doesn't add anything to the quilt, and I want the quilting to create the next level of design. Also, if you pressed the seam allowances open and stitched right in the seamline, you could pierce through and cut the thread used for the patchwork. I don't always quilt around all the units. I might outline just a star, for example, or just part of the block.

- **Quilt an entirely different design.** You can use straight-line quilting to add another design over the block, disregarding the lines of the patchwork. For example, you might want to stitch from corner to corner on the block and then intersect the diagonal lines with additional lines, creating a new design level on your quilt.

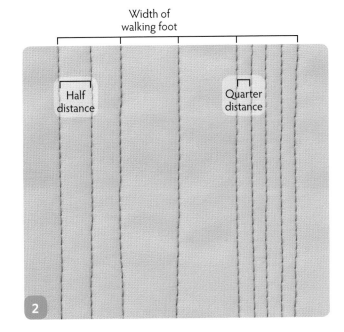

Width of walking foot

Half distance

Quarter distance

2

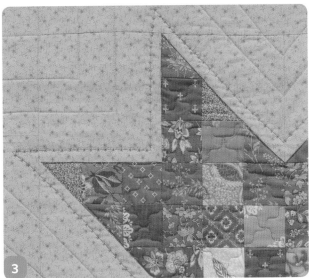

3

Plan on Paper First

Draw a few designs on paper to see what look you like and determine if your idea will be easy enough to stitch. You'll have to turn your whole quilt each time you need to stitch in a different direction, which can be a bit more tedious if you need turn a lot. In that case, outlining might be easier with free-motion quilting.

Tips for Straight-Line Quilting

- **Try using a guide bar** for equal spacing. Many machines have a guide bar that you attach to your walking foot. The guide bar allows you to sew evenly spaced lines, and you can adjust the distance by sliding the bar to the right or left.

- **If you're getting puckering** along the stitched lines, see if you can decrease the amount of pressure on the walking foot so there's less pressure on the fabric layers. That usually fixes the problem. If you can't adjust the pressure on your walking foot, you can alleviate puckers by either sewing lines in opposite directions, making your stitch length a little longer, or sewing the lines farther apart. Use a test sample to determine what works.

- **When stitching lines close together** in an outer border, try to avoid creating puckers along the outer edges of the quilt by ending ½" from the edge.

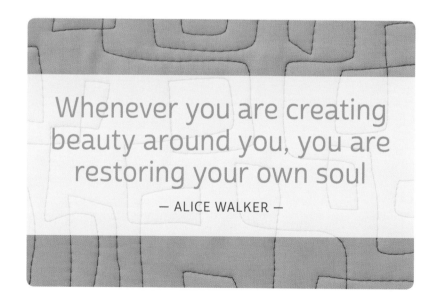

Whenever you are creating beauty around you, you are restoring your own soul

— ALICE WALKER —

DECORATIVE STITCHES, CIRCLES, AND CURVES

You can use decorative stitches to easily stitch circles and curves with the aid of a walking foot. Each of these can add a super fun look to your quilt.

Wave Stitch

I love the wave stitch; stitching it from edge to edge is a nice alternative to a straight line. I can make it wide, or long and slender. If your machine has this stitch option, try varying the size to see what you like for your project.

- **Line 1.** Stitch width is 6.5 mm and stitch length is 2.0 mm. If you want the line to be less curvy, increase the stitch length.

- **Line 2.** Stitch width is 6.5 mm and stitch length is 4.5 mm. To create a slightly more open curve, decrease the stitch width and use a shorter stitch length.

- **Line 3.** Stitch width is 5.0 mm and stitch length is 2.0 mm.

- **Line 4.** To make a more compact line of stitches, set the stitch width to 4.0 mm and stitch length to 1.0 mm. Keep in mind that this compact line of curves will take longer to complete.

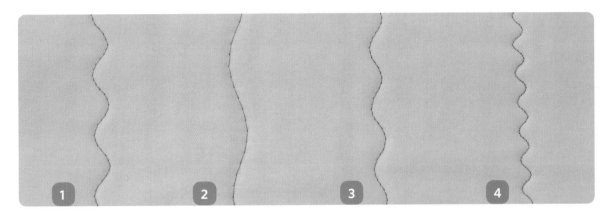

Decorative Stitches

Look for decorative stitches that are more open in style rather than ones that are dense and have filled-in areas. It's easier to stitch through all the layers using these types of stitches, and they don't take as long to do. Use a sample quilt sandwich to test the stitches to see how they look. You may need to elongate the stitch to handle the quilt sandwich. Your machine may have a lot of these fun stitches, including vines with berries, flowers, snowflakes, and even cars and trains! The stitches shown below are available on the Baby Lock Crescendo. Your machine may have similar options.

6-078   6-089   6-088   6-058

Circles and Spirals

Starting in the center of the quilt, stitch a circle and then use the edge of your walking foot as a guide to stitch slowly around and around to create a spiral that covers the entire quilt. I find that it works best to stitch circles slowly when using a walking foot.

1. Draw a circle on the uncoated side of a piece of freezer paper. The size of the circle depends on the size of your project. I use a 3½"-diameter circle on smaller projects and a 4½"-diameter circle on larger ones. Press the shiny side of the freezer-paper circle onto the quilt top where you want to start the spiral, or trace the circle using a water-soluble marker. If you're centering the circle on the quilt top, fold the freezer-paper circle into quarters with the shiny side out. Align the center creases with the center of the quilt top and either trace around the circle or press it in place.

2. Along the edge of the circle, make two marks about 1½" to 2" apart **(photo 1).**

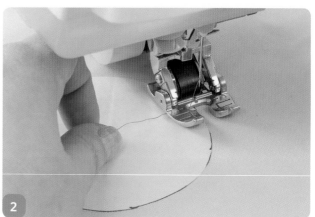

3. Start stitching at the second mark; the first mark will be behind the needle **(photo 2).** Stitch very close to the freezer-paper circle. If you drew the line, stitch directly on the line.

4. Stop stitching about halfway around the circle and place a straight pin ½" from the second mark (the mark where you started quilting) as shown **(photo 3).** When you reach the first mark, start angling away from the circle and head toward the pin to start a spiral. As you reach the pin, remove it and align the edge of your walking foot with the stitched line.

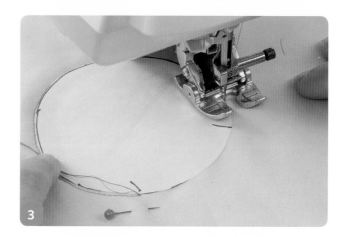

5. Continue stitching, aligning the edge of your walking foot with the stitched line. Stitch full circles around and around until you reach the edges of the quilt top.

6. When you reach the outer edges, stitch partial circles **(photo 4)** to complete the design in the quilt's corners.

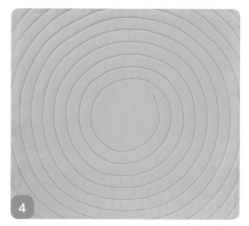

Curves

You can build an overall design that complements your quilt top. I love doing this in an organic way—stitching one section and then adding another.

1. **Sketch a design.** I like to make a sketch to get the flow of the design **(photo 1).** When I start stitching, I keep the sketch nearby as a reference. Remember, the design is organic, so don't worry about following the sketch exactly. Just use it as a guide.

2. **To determine how many stitches** you'll need to sew before turning, measure the number of stitches between the needle and the edge of the walking foot. In this example, it's about eight stitches. So, when you reach the side of the sample, stop with the needle in the down position, pivot the quilt, and stitch eight stitches along the edge of the sample.

3. **Stop and pivot again.** Start stitching a curve in the opposite direction, a walking-foot distance from the previously stitched line **(photo 2).**

4. **Continue in the same way,** filling the sample with stitched curves **(photo 3).**

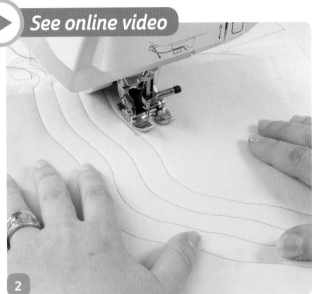

See online video

See Pat demonstrate quilting curved lines with a walking foot at ShopMartingale.com/PatSloanVideos

Appliqué and Quilting Combined

For smaller quilts that have just a touch of appliqué, I like using a walking foot to blanket-stitch around the appliqué shape, sewing through all three layers. This means I'm also quilting around the shape, so I'll need less quilting later. Since I have to turn the entire piece, with all three layers, this technique is not easy to use on a large quilt. However, it's perfect for smaller projects, such as table runners and wall hangings.

1. **Fuse your shapes** to the background fabric. Then baste the quilt as described on page 12.

2. **Using an open-toe walking foot,** blanket-stitch around the appliqué shape **(photo 1).**

3. **Mark a straight line** on one side of the shape, close to the edge of the shape. Stitch a straight line. I used painter's tape and stitched on both sides of the tape **(photo 2).** Stitch additional lines as needed until you reach the edge of the quilt sandwich.

4. **To fill in above and below** the appliqué, stitch evenly spaced straight lines, stopping when you reach the shape. Start stitching again on the other side of the shape. If you're jumping a short distance, such as inside where the cat's tail curls, simply stop with a locking stitch, jump over the shape, and then start with a locking stitch and sew to the outer edge **(photo 3).** When you reach the outer edge, stop with a locking stitch and clip the threads.

5. **Last, stitch evenly spaced lines** on the other side of the shape.

Backing Fabric

Blanket stitches will show on the back of the quilt. If you use a busy print with lots of colors for the backing, the stitches will be less noticeable.

1

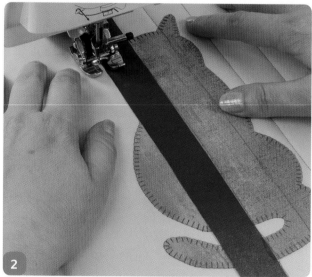

2

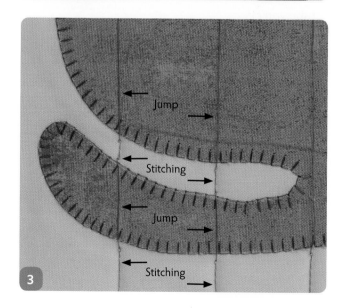

Jump

Stitching

Jump

Stitching

3

Locking Blocks in Place

When I'm quilting a larger quilt constructed of multiple blocks joined into rows, I start by stitching along the block lines to make a large grid. Stitching a grid locks the three layers together and allows me to remove some of the basting pins, which makes it easier to quilt the blocks.

- **If the blocks are 12" x 12",** the grid might be as small as the blocks. I usually stitch in the ditch between all the block rows, horizontally and vertically. For smaller blocks, such as those that are 6" square, the stitched lines might be as far apart as two rows and two columns of blocks, or one block and sashing.

- **Stitch about ⅛" from the seam.** Stitching just to the side of the seam instead of "in the ditch" makes a stronger bond **(photo 1).**

- **Using a thread color that blends** with the fabrics will make the stitches less noticeable **(photo 2).**

Density of Quilting

Density refers to how close together your quilting lines appear. Depending on the fiber type and how the batting is made, you may be able to quilt lines as far apart as 8", or you may need to quilt them much closer together to make sure that when you launder the quilt the batting holds together as intended. Be sure to use the minimum required distance for the batting you choose.

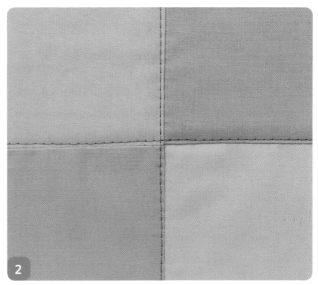

Think about how much time you want to spend quilting the project. The more quilting you add, the more time it takes. If the quilt doesn't need lots of quilting, you can finish it quicker by using the minimum required distance.

The other big factor in quilting density is consistency. If you heavily quilt one area, such as the center of a star, you need to balance the rest of the quilting so the density is the same in all areas, including the border, or the quilt will not be flat.

Handling the Quilt

- **Fluff and scrunch the quilt.** I don't roll a quilt. I find that taking an organic approach and having the quilt piled up on my table makes it easier to handle **(photo 1)**.

- **Never let the quilt fall off the table.** The key to working with a large quilt is to keep the entire quilt on the table surface and not let it fall off the edges so it doesn't pull or drag. Once it falls off, the weight makes it hard to move the quilt.

- **Turning the quilt.** With a walking foot, you have less freedom of motion for turning. With smaller quilts, turning isn't too hard to handle. But for larger quilts, there's a lot of bulk to deal with. I work best when I have a plan and know what type of straight-line quilting I'm doing. I make a sketch for reference and use it to look ahead and see where I need to turn next.

- **Managing a large quilt.** It can be a challenge to manage a large quilt. For tips to make it easier, see "Large-Quilt Management" on page 45.

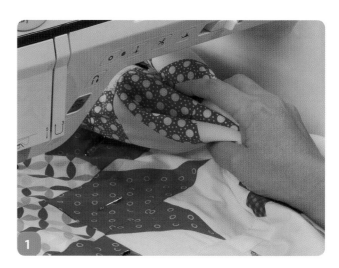

Planning Straight-Line Designs

Our minds are very powerful learners. When we practice drawing quilt designs, we create what is known as muscle memory. Our brain starts to learn the motion we are making with our hand and arm. Later when we go to quilt that design, we kick into autopilot and it's much easier to make those same motions. Muscle memory is why you can still ride a bike even if you haven't been on one for years. As soon as you get on the seat, put your hands on the handlebars, and place your feet on the pedals, your brain remembers what to do.

With the amazing Internet where people are sharing their work, we're able to see so many quilts and quilting options. Start looking at quilts to see how they're quilted. And I don't mean just basic quilting; look at complicated and fancy quilting too. You might see a design element that can be a starting point for an overall pattern or part of a block. Floor tiles and wallpaper also have lots of line drawings that are inspiration for quilting patterns.

Let's look at some ways to try out quilting designs in advance.

- **Print a black-and-white image** of your quilt and draw designs on top of the printed image.

- **Place a clear acetate sheet** on top of your quilt. (Acetate sheets range from 9" x 12" to 19" x 24" and can cover a small quilt or a section of a larger quilt.) Draw your designs on the acetate using a dry-erase marker, being careful not to accidently draw on your quilt.

- **If you like to use your computer,** as I do, scan a photo of the quilt top into a photo-editor program. There are programs on the Internet you can use for free. Use the pencil tool to draw a quilting design on top of the image. Then save the photo for reference.

- **Keep a sketchbook.** Doodling in a spiral sketchbook lets you build a portfolio of shapes to use when you start planning a quilting design. It also builds your memory for the shapes.

Advice If You Don't Want to Practice

For straight-line quilting, you really can jump right in and start quilting a project. But I have a few suggestions so you will be happy with the results right away!

- **Start with a project that is not precious.** Don't start on a quilt that you spent a year piecing. Instead, make one of the quick projects from this book and quilt it. Or, start with a quilt top you already have that didn't take very long to make.

- **Quilt an edge-to-edge design first.** This allows you to practice handling a larger quilt and getting a feel for how that works. You'll also learn how your walking foot operates and what to expect from it.

- **Stop procrastinating.** You'll make more quilts. So, quilt a few that are less precious, and then move up to those amazing quilt tops and turn them into finished quilts!

Professional Quilting

How do I decide when to send a quilt top out for quilting? I don't quilt all my own quilts. Sometimes I have tight deadlines, so I'll send a quilt to someone else to have it quilted. Sometimes I don't want to use my time to quilt a bed-sized project and will have someone else quilt a nice edge-to-edge design. And other times, I want my talented friends to add their level of art to my quilt top. I have friends with an incredible eye for quilt designs. These quilters make my projects amazing with their added quilting designs. So I decide on a case-by-case basis, depending on the time I have available and the level of artistry I want.

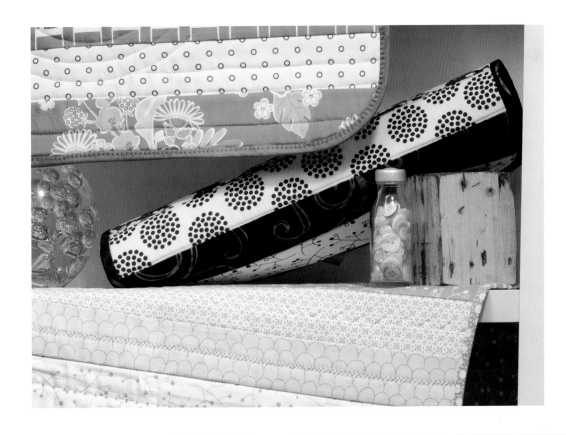

Free-Motion Machine Quilting

When I learned to quilt, I knew I wanted to create swirls and curves on my pieces. That can only be done with free-motion quilting. When you lower the feed dogs on your machine, you can move your quilt in any direction you like to make the stitches. This method of quilting gives you so many more design options to add to your quilt. I'm sure you've been to quilt shows or looked around online and seen amazing quilting. You can do quilting like that too, once you learn the basics of controlling your stitches.

With free-motion quilting, you can follow shapes (appliqués or motifs in the fabric), stitch background fills, and create interesting designs on your quilt top. In this book, I'm giving you a foundation so you'll have the basics mastered.

But first, take a deep breath. Free-motion quilting is not scary, but you'll probably make some scary-looking stitches before you figure it all out. Accept that you won't be an expert at the beginning, and it will be much easier to learn. Your quilting may not be perfect until you've done a few projects. That's normal! It's how we all learn and become better. If you can relax about this part, you'll find that your quilting will become better much faster. Why? Because quilting several pieces builds muscle memory, and then the motions become easier. You'll soon be creating wonderful stitches, so believe in yourself and it will all happen much quicker, I promise.

Now, let's get started!

Start with a Sandwich

Just as with walking-foot quilting, you'll need to prepare your quilt sandwich by basting the backing, batting, and quilt top together with safety pins or basting spray. Try to pin in areas you're less likely to quilt; otherwise you'll need to remove the pins as you go so you don't stitch into them. See "Getting Ready to Machine Quilt" on page 8 for all the details on prepping your quilt.

> Everyone who got where he is has had to begin where he was.
>
> — ROBERT LOUIS STEVENSON —

What You'll Need

Darning foot. For free-motion quilting, you'll use a darning foot, which is also called a free-motion foot or pogo foot **(photo 1).** It comes in metal or plastic, depending on your machine brand. The metal types are often open in the front, making a C shape. This is called an "open-toe darning foot." They're also available with a closed toe, which makes the foot a full circle or oval. I use a metal open-toe foot for better visibility, because I want to watch just ahead of where I'm currently stitching. Regardless of the material it's made from or whether it's open or closed, the darning foot has a built-in spring so that when you stitch, the foot hops up and down. That gives you the freedom to move the quilt layers under the needle as you sew. When the needle goes up the foot hops up, and you can move the quilt—forward, backward, side to side, in circles, or however you choose.

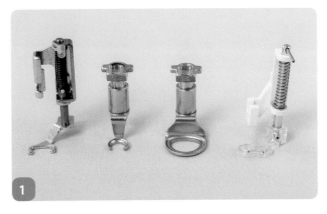

Gloves. Made just for free-motion quilting, these specialty gloves are thin and lightweight, with small rubber grippers on the ends of the fingertips **(photo 2).** Not everyone likes wearing gloves to quilt, but I recommend trying them to see if they help you move the quilt more freely.

Surface cover. To make it easier to move your quilt as you sew, you may find that a cover for your machine bed is in order **(photo 2).** These sheets are made of Teflon or silicone and help your quilt sandwich glide over the surface with very little friction. This may not be critical for a small project, but when quilting a larger quilt, having less drag will be appreciated.

Small scissors. Keep these handy to snip threads as you go **(photo 2).** You don't want those thread tails getting tangled in your stitching.

Free-Motion Lessons

Let's go over the basics, from starting and stopping to regulating the length of your stitches. Then we'll move on to troubleshooting (just in case!) and the various styles of free-motion designs you might want to try.

STARTING

1. If you have a needle up/down button on your machine, select the needle-down position so that every time you stop stitching, the needle will be down in the quilt sandwich. You do this to secure your work so it won't shift when you stop.

2. Drop the feed dogs. The feed dogs on your machine are the parallel set of jagged teeth that move back and forth as you sew. With free-motion quilting, you don't want the feed dogs to move or grab the fabric as you maneuver the quilt. That's going to be *your* job! Lower the feed dogs (see your machine manual if you're not sure how to do this) so the quilt can flow freely, and then you'll be in control **(photo 1)**. On some machines, it's possible to quilt quite nicely with the feed dogs up, which some people prefer. Try it both ways to see which way is best for you.

3. Lower the presser foot. Using the needle up/down button or the foot pedal, sink the needle down into the fabric and then let it come all the way back up. Gently tug the thread tail until the bobbin thread loops up through the surface of the quilt sandwich **(photo 2)**. Grab the loop and pull on it until the bobbin tail is all the way on the surface.

4. Holding onto the top and bobbin threads, position them to the back of the presser foot **(photo 3)**. This keeps the threads from creating a mess on the back of the quilt when you start running the machine.

5. Take several stitches in place to lock the threads. (Remember, the feed dogs won't be moving the fabric, so if you don't move the quilt with your hands, you can easily take a few stitches in one place just by putting your foot on the machine's pedal.)

6. After quilting for an inch, stop and trim the threads at the surface of the quilt. Or, after you finish quilting an area, knot the threads and bury them in the batting layer using a hand-sewing needle **(photo 4)**.

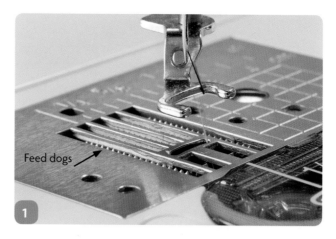

Feed dogs

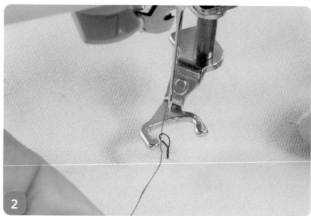

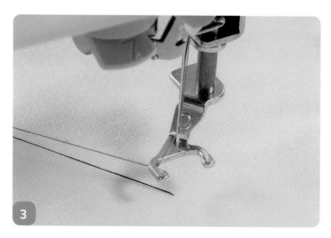

STOPPING

1. **To end, take several stitches** in place to lock the threads. Trim the threads at the surface. An alternate method is to tie a knot and then bury the thread tails in the batting **(photo 1)** using a hand-sewing needle.

2. **If you run out of bobbin thread,** tie off the threads on the back of the quilt and weave the tails into the batting. For details on how to do this, see "Running Out of Bobbin Thread" on page 20. Start stitching again where you left off.

CONTROLLING SPEED

Since the feed dogs are not engaged, *you* are in charge of moving the quilt around under the needle to create the design. Sounds easy enough. But the secret to good free-motion quilting is this: *even hand motion = consistent stitches.*

Yep, that's it. To make nice even-length stitches, you need to move your quilt around at an even pace. The goal is to run the machine at a speed that matches the motion of your hands so that your stitches are an even length. This is your number-one item to master. It takes practice (see "Practice Routinely" on page 47), but you can do this!

So, how do you know if your hands are moving at the right speed? Let's look at two examples.

If your stitches are too long **(photo 2),** you're moving the quilt faster than you are sewing. The solution? Either run the machine faster or slow the speed of your hands. Try both and see which works best for you.

Conversely, if your stitches are very short **(photo 3),** you're running the risk of damaging the fabric by piercing it too close together with the machine needle. To fix this, either move the quilt more quickly with your hands or slow the machine speed. (Frankly, it's a bit easier to slow the machine!) See "Controlling the Machine Speed" at right.

The sweet spot is when you find a steady pace to run the machine and the correct speed to move the quilt sandwich **(photo 4).** This will eventually become second nature. I share some tips on pages 36 and 37 to get you to this spot faster!

▶ *See online video*

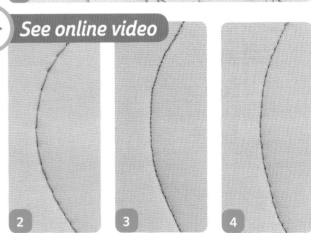

See Pat demonstrate controlling stitching speed at ShopMartingale.com/PatSloanVideos

Controlling the Machine Speed

Many machines have a speed control, which will help you maintain a consistent sewing speed. The control may be a slider on the front of the machine or a half-speed button. This feature allows you to sew pedal-to-the-metal while the machine goes only the max speed you set. Using this feature can be helpful when free-motion quilting, because you may find it easier to push the foot pedal all the way down rather than pushing it only partway and trying to maintain that speed. It also may be less fatiguing for your foot and leg.

LEARNING TO CONTROL YOUR STITCH LENGTH

Whether or not your machine has a speed regulator, you need to learn to control the length of your stitches and try to keep them uniform. You don't need to strive for perfection—none of us can attain that! Just shoot for a stitch length you like. Minor imperfections won't be visible or impact the overall look of your finished quilt. Honest!

Running the foot speed and moving your hands to match it for consistent stitches takes practice, but you will become attuned to this by doing it over and over. You build your muscle memory by actually quilting. It won't happen by reading about it. Nor will that memory happen if you only quilt for an hour once a month. You need to do the work and quilt things. So let's quilt a sample so you can figure out your go-to mode.

1. **Make three to six 18" x 20"** test quilt sandwiches with a top, backing, and batting. I recommend using solid fabrics for the top and backing so you can see your stitches. Baste the three layers for use in this series of exercises.

2. **Using a notebook,** practice drawing swirls **(photo 1).** You're striving for smooth curves, and drawing swirl after swirl is perfect for creating a memory of that motion as you use your mind and hands.

3. **Place one of your test quilt sandwiches** under the needle of your machine. Lower the feed dogs and presser foot. You might like having the drawing of your design next to the machine so you can see it and know where you're going. Pull up your bobbin thread and make a locking stitch.

4. **Start slowly,** setting your speed regulator to the lowest it can go (if you have this feature). If your *machine* runs *slowly,* then your *hands* must *also* move *slowly.* Start stitching swirls—just like those in your drawing. Your goal is to move your hands at a consistent speed to create a consistent stitch length **(photo 2).** Write "slow speed" next to these stitches on the sample background fabric.

See online video

See Pat demonstrate drawing swirl designs at ShopMartingale.com/PatSloanVideos

Draw First, Sew Later!

I recommend drawing a design on paper before stitching it on your machine the first time. When learning a design, it's much easier to make the shapes even and uniform on paper, so take an organic approach. Right now you want to learn the motion and become consistent. Mastering a design on your machine comes later.

5. Next, set your speed control to the middle speed (or sew at a medium speed by pressing the foot pedal only halfway down as you go) **(photo 3).** When sewing at a medium speed, you must move your hands a little faster or you'll create teeny tiny stitches. Sew some swirls on this setting and write "medium speed" on the fabric.

6. **Now sew at a very fast speed** to see how you like it. I have more control running the machine faster, but everyone's experience is different. Stitch some swirls and mark this as "top speed" on the fabric.

7. **If you've been using a speed regulator** to control your machine speed, go back and try the slow, medium, and fast speeds on your own. Using just the pressure on the foot pedal to control your speed, stitch new samples and label them "manual, slow" (or "manual, medium" or "manual, fast").

8. **Think about which method** was most comfortable. Did you prefer setting the speed regulator and putting your pedal all the way down? Or did you like the control of pushing the pedal only as far as you need to? Choose the option that's most comfortable for you, and then practice, practice, practice!

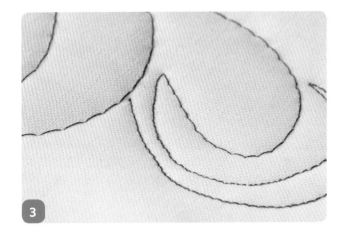

3

The Right Stitch Length

As you look at different quilts, you'll see stitch lengths that vary from ⅟₁₆" to ⅛" long, depending on the quilter, the project, and even the area of the quilt. One person might love very tiny stitches, and another might like them a bit bigger. **Being consistent is what is important.** *Pick a length you like. Then strive to stitch that length on a consistent basis. Your goal is to have a machine speed and hand speed that is consistent and will produce the stitch length you want.*

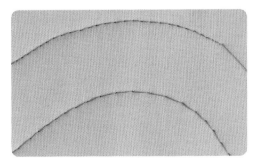

Stitch lengths: top, ⅟₁₆"; bottom, ⅛"

Correcting Stitch-Tension Problems

Even with as much care and attention as you take to follow all the steps for good free-motion quilting, undoubtedly a pesky problem will come up now and then. Here's a look at what to strive for and also a description of some common situations and what to do about them.

The stitches on the top and back of your quilt should look the same. The ends of each stitch should sink into the fabric. The top or bobbin thread should *not* simply lie on the surface. There should also be no loops or pulling.

To fix general tension problems, try the following solutions in this order:

- Put in a new needle.

- Rethread the machine.

- Be sure your top and bobbin threads are the same brand and weight.

- Clean out the lint from under your feed dogs and around the bobbin casing.

- Make sure the feed dogs are lowered.

- Test the tension again.

Now let's look at specific problems to see how you can fix them.

Problem: Pulling or "eyelashes" around curves **(photo 1).** Having lovely eyelashes may be something we all strive for—but not on our quilts! If the stitches are pulling when you're quilting curves (on the quilt top or back), you need to stop and fix the problem.

Solution: Pulling is the number-one problem people have with free-motion quilting, and it's rarely caused by poor thread tension. It's usually an issue of getting the speed of the machine and the motion of our hands in sync for great stitches. The first thing to do when you see this issue is test your hand speed and machine speed. Most likely they're not working together so you're pulling the needle, which causes poor stitches.

Perfect tension

Disguising Little Tension Issues

It's very difficult to maintain perfect thread tension all the time, so match the top and bobbin thread color. That way, if the bobbin thread pops to the top or vice versa, the thread won't be noticeable.

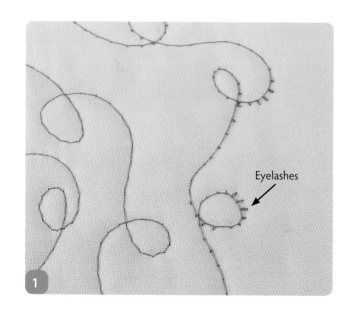

1

Eyelashes

Look at the quilt. Are you getting more loops on the curve? Then you're speeding up the motion of your hands as you get to the curve. The solution is to be aware of that and *not* speed up your hands. Or, if you move the fabric faster, run the machine faster to maintain the same ratio of hand speed to machine speed.

Start quilting a lot of curves and either move your hands slower or the run the machine faster. You'll see a difference either way. You may find that you want to speed up the machine only when you stitch loops. That's fine. The goal is consistent stitches, so do what feels natural and comfortable to accomplish that.

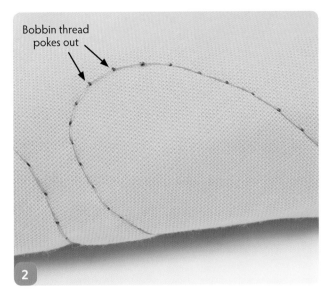

Problem: The top thread lies flat on the surface and the bobbin thread is looped over it **(photo 2).**

Solution: Loosen or lower the top-thread tension one number at a time, testing each time until the tension is correct.

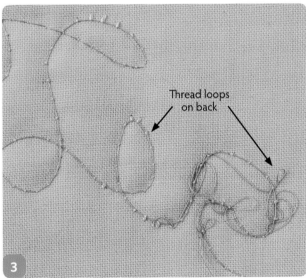

Problem: The top thread is fine, but when you flip the quilt over, there are thread loops on the back **(photo 3).**

Solution: Tighten or increase the top-thread tension one number at a time, testing each time until the tension is correct.

Fiddle with the bobbin case as a last resort. The screw on the bobbin case is tiny. To adjust the bobbin tension, turn the screw only about ⅛" or less at a time, and then test the tension again.

If you're still having trouble, take your samples to your local sewing machine dealer and ask for troubleshooting help.

Stitching Styles

Often when people first start learning about machine quilting, someone mentions stippling, and then beginners think that's the only type of free-motion quilting they can do. Stippling is simply a style or type of quilting. It means stitching very small meandering lines and never crossing over them. Stippling can be large in scale or very small. There are strict rules about how it should look to be called stippling.

Luckily, that's not the only way to machine quilt. When I first started quilting my own projects, nobody had mentioned any rules, so I did my own thing. I stitched little swirls and loops, I crossed the lines (gasp!), and had a lot of fun. Now, free-motion quilting consists of an amazing array of styles. You may hear terms like stippling, meandering, allover designs, curves, loops, background fills, bubbles, feathers, and geometrics. These are all styles of quilting, and you can use just one or combine a number of them—it's all up to you.

In this book, I'll share a group of styles that will build your skill level and expertise. After you're comfortable with these designs, you can expand your skills with many other styles, and maybe create your own!

HOW TO APPROACH ANY BASIC DESIGN

One thing that will make building your own library of shapes easy and fun is learning how to approach the stitching direction of a design. Let's look at the thought process for several shapes, building from simple shapes to ones with more directions. When you draw the shapes on paper, you learn the direction and motion needed before going to the machine.

Stitch these basic fills on a quilt sandwich to develop your own stitch rhythm and style.

- **Simple repeat loop.** Stitch a line for an inch or more, then "draw" the loop with your needle, making big, medium, and small loops. At the end of a loop, you can continue in the same direction or change directions before you make another loop **(fig. 1).**

- **Angular shapes like boxes and rectangles.** When stitching angular shapes, change directions more often. I think of these shapes as random angles that sometimes overlap. By drawing them on paper, I can plan how often I want to change directions so I don't have all the boxes going in a straight line **(fig. 2).**

Fig. 1

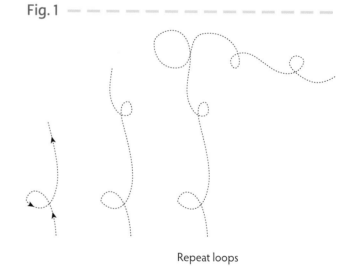

Repeat loops

Fig. 2

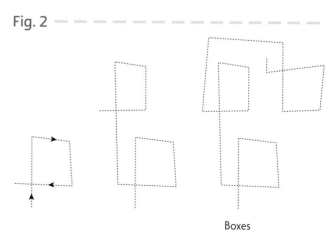

Boxes

- **Echo.** An echo is an outline of a shape already on the quilt, whether it's appliquéd or a design on the fabric. Outline the shape, which makes an echo of the shape. You can stitch it once or repeat the outline a few times **(fig. 3)**.

- **Bounce and echo.** A bounce and echo work together to first outline a shape, and then make a new shape. I find echoing a curve or a teardrop shape is the easiest way to start. Stitch the initial teardrop shape. Then echo the shape two or three times. At the end of the last echo, rotate the piece and stitch a new teardrop. Repeat to fill in an area **(fig. 4)**.

Most shapes that you can sketch can be machine quilted. Practicing these designs will hone your skills, so if you decide to try more detailed shapes, you'll know how to think about them. Let's look at these ideas stitched on fabric.

MEANDERING, LOOPS, AND SWIRLS

I group all three of these styles together, because using all three in conjunction is often my go-to style for quilting an allover design **(photo 1).** I might stitch them across a whole quilt, as background fill behind appliqué, or right over the top of a pieced block. If my quilt has sashing, I may change up the quilting and stitch something different in the sashing so that I can quilt loops and swirls in one small area at a time. Sometimes I'll add little shapes such as leaves, hearts, stars, and flowers to my loops and swirls.

SHARP LINES—RECTANGLES, TRIANGLES, AND SQUARES

Geometric shapes are fun to stitch side by side or stacked and overlapping **(photo 2).** I like to use them on quilts for guys, because sometimes flowery loops and swirls don't fit the bill. Sharp lines are also fun to use within a pieced block to give it extra texture.

Remember, you aren't turning your quilt to make box designs—you're moving your quilt in different directions. So you'll be sewing toward yourself, to the right, away from yourself, and then to the left. The lines don't need to be perfectly straight, and

Fig. 3

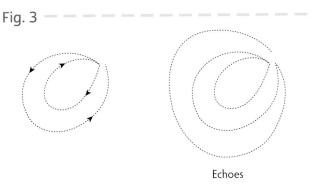

Echoes

Fig. 4

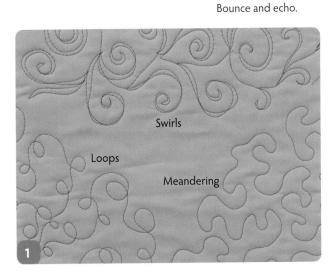

Bounce and echo.

Swirls

Loops

Meandering

1

2

the corners don't need to be right angles to achieve the desired effect. To make sharp turns **(photo 3)**, always stop at the end of a stitched line with the needle down in the fabric. Pause, and then switch stitching direction. This way, whatever angle the corners form, they're bound to be nice and sharp.

ECHOING CURVY SHAPES

To make a teardrop, start where you want the pointed end to be. Stitch a line that curves out slightly, and then swoop around the wide curved end and come back to the point. Echo the shape, using the width of the presser foot as a spacer. The shapes can be clustered, bounced off each other, and done in combination with other shapes **(photo 4).**

QUILTING APPLIQUÉ

To me, it's easier to think of free-motion designs for appliqué quilts than for pieced quilts. I have a 1-2-3 solution for quilting appliqué.

1. **Outline stitch** around all the appliqué shapes, including stems, leaves, flowers, and other shapes, stitching as close to the edge of the appliqué as you can **(photo 5)**.

2. **Quilt a background fill** to flatten the background and give it texture, such as bubbles **(photo 5).** This allows the appliqué to pop off the surface.

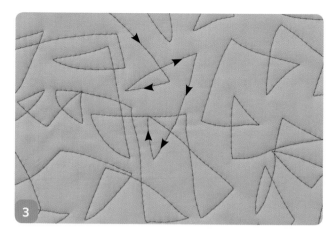

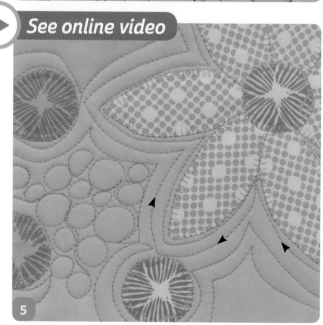

See Pat demonstrate quilting bubbles at ShopMartingale.com/PatSloanVideos

3. Accent larger appliqué shapes with some quilting **(photo 6).** Add a vein to a leaf, stitch a design in a basket, make roof tiles on a house, and so on. Some people don't like to quilt on top of appliqué, but you need to quilt big shapes because you don't want to leave large areas of the quilt unquilted.

QUILTING INSIDE APPLIQUÉ SHAPES

When I quilt an appliqué piece, I handle quilting inside the shapes in two different ways.

Option 1. Use the same thread you're using to quilt the background **(photo 6).** For the snowman, I quilted his body using the same blue thread I used in the background. Find a spot on the appliqué shape where you can smoothly transition from the background into the shape, quilt the shape, and then stitch back onto the background at the same spot where you started.

Option 2. Change the thread color to match the appliqué **(photo 7).** Plan ahead so you can quilt all the appliqués that require the same color, and then change colors and move on to the next batch. For example, if you're quilting leaves, stitch all the leaves before changing to another color to quilt flowers or other motifs.

6

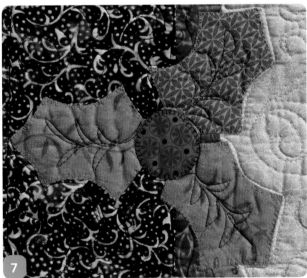

7

Wash Your Quilt

After the binding is attached, wash your quilt. Washing pulls together all the lovely fabrics, batting, and threads to make a piece you'll love. It's the perfect ending to a quilt.

QUILTING PIECED BLOCKS

Sketching ideas on a black-and-white image or a digitally drawn block will help you have a plan for the pieced block. Make multiple copies so you can draw several ideas to see what you like best.

1. **If your blocks are set side by side,** you might want to quilt more than one type of design in neighboring blocks **(photo 8).**

2. **If there's sashing** between the blocks, I use a simple wave design to quilt it **(photo 9).**

3. **When moving from one area** to another, such as from one block to another with sashing between the blocks, sew a few locking stitches in place. Raise the needle out of the fabric, lift the presser foot (I call this a "jump"), and then move the quilt so that the next area to work on will be under the needle. Lower the presser foot, sew a couple of locking stitches, and you're ready to start again.

QUILTING STRAIGHT LINES

It's harder to stitch straight lines with free-motion quilting than with a walking foot, but it's not impossible **(photo 10).** Look ahead to where you want to go and move the quilt toward yourself for best control when stitching straight lines. Of course, for some projects, you may find it easier to use a combination of free-motion and walking-foot quilting. I switch to a walking foot for long straight lines, like along the edge of sashing or an inner border.

Take Little Jumps

When I jump from one area to another, I don't move very far, just a few inches. I start again with a locking stitch and then keep going. After I've stitched a little distance, I carefully trim the threads close to the surface at the starting and stopping points to avoid having the presser foot get tangled in the thread.

See online video

See Pat demonstrate combining walking-foot and free-motion quilting at ShopMartingale.com/PatSloanVideos

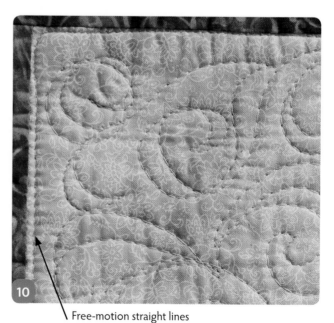

Free-motion straight lines

Handling a Quilt

It's one thing to practice quilting on smaller quilt sandwiches, but transitioning to a large quilt can take some adjusting. How do you manage all the bulk? Where do you start quilting? Not to worry. I have pointers for you!

LARGE-QUILT MANAGEMENT

Handling a large quilt is a mental game. To make it easier, keep in mind that you need to have only a bit more than half of the quilt in the throat (or harp) space. When you turn the quilt, you'll deal with the other half.

I don't roll the quilt to get it out of my way. Instead, I fluff and scrunch a quilt as I work **(photo 1).** Working in an organic way and having the quilt piled up on my sewing table makes it easier to handle. The key to working with a large quilt is never to let it fall off the table. Once it falls off the edge of the table, you can't move it freely. So keep the entire quilt on the table surface.

Maneuvering a larger quilt is much easier when free-motion quilting than when using a walking foot. You can sew sideways, backward, and forward. Sometimes you may need to turn the quilt for specific designs, but most of the time you can quilt from one section right into the next, no turning required.

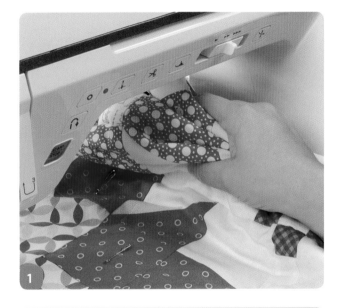

WHERE TO START QUILTING

For any quilt, it's a good idea to plan your approach to your quilting before you begin. For a big quilt, this is very important. You'll also want to think about how dense the quilting will be. For more about density of quilting, see page 29.

If your quilt is basted well (and it should be! see page 12 for more on basting), you can start any place you like on the quilt. That said, I do have some preferences I've developed over the years. No matter what type of quilting I'm doing, if the quilt is large, I like to start in the middle. I complete the middle section first, because quilting the middle of a large quilt is the most tedious part. There is more bulk to handle, more to manage. Once the middle has been quilted, the rest of the quilt is easier to do.

Allover designs. Start at the edge of the quilt and work toward the middle. Then stitch toward the other side, working from edge to edge, but don't travel in a straight line. Use more of a wandering design so the quilting has an organic feel **(photo 2).**

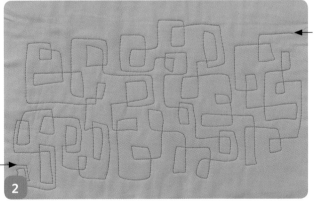

I started quilting at the left arrow and ended at the right arrow.

Block-based designs. On each block, start at a spot that has a bit of a straight area so you can warm up to the design before making turns **(photo 3)**. For example, on the center plus shape, I started at the top left of the shape and stitched the width of the shape before turning.

Appliqué. Outline stitch around the appliqué shapes, stitch the background fill, and then stitch inside the shapes (see "Quilting Appliqué" on page 42) **(photo 4)**.

What-to-Quilt Overview

The question I'm asked the most is this: "What do I quilt?" I approach my work by having the go-to designs in my repertoire that we explored earlier (stippling, loops, triangles, rectangles, and so on). Then I collect ideas that I'd like to try out for future use. Here are a few ways to keep ideas for later.

- **Use books and magazines** for ideas. Many have close-ups of quilting designs so you can see what the quilter did.

- **Peruse websites of quilt designers you like,** and see how these experts quilt their projects. Or log onto sites such as Flickr and Pinterest, where you can view many quilts. Don't just look at the colors and patchwork—check out the quilting! If you're on Pinterest, make a board to keep all your favorite quilting photos, so you can refer to them each time you're getting ready to quilt a project. It's fun and inspirational.

- **When you're at a quilt show,** look at quilting styles. Note why you're drawn to a particular style and what you like about it. Take photos (if allowed; ask for permission) and keep them in a digital album. Put a note with each design. Later when you're ready to do your quilting, look through the album for inspiration.

- **Practice free-motion quilting designs** by sketching them in a notebook. Draw shapes and fill them in with quilting ideas **(photo 5)**. Draw quilt blocks and create free-motion designs over the top of them. This has the bonus of building your muscle memory so the process is easier each time.

- **Take a photo** or digital image of a pieced block and doodle different ways of quilting right on the block layout.

Practice Routinely

I can't say it enough. Practice is what makes free-motion quilting your friend. You need to quilt frequently to build muscle memory so that free-motion quilting becomes second nature. Can you remember the first time you got in a car and had to figure out how to control the speed (like the sewing machine's foot pedal), watch where you were going (like your quilting line), and do those two things at the same time while changing the radio station? There's no radio on your sewing machine, so it'll be easier. Just don't run into anyone!

Driving took practice until many of those motions became automatic. Before long, you didn't have to concentrate to control the speed, and eventually you didn't have to remind yourself to look for traffic–plus you added more tasks. This was all possible because you drove your car over and over and over again.

In the beginning of this book, I mentioned that I'd give you a way to practice on real things. For walking-foot quilting, it's pretty easy to jump right in. Start with a quilt top that is not so precious and you're on your way. But for free-motion quilting, you need to cut yourself some slack. You need to practice when you first start free-motion quilting or if it's been a while since you last quilted. You need a warm-up piece. So I've devised a plan, and I promise that if you do my 5-step plan, you'll see a huge improvement in your quilting skills from quilt 1 to quilt 5.

BECOMING A BETTER QUILTER IN FIVE EASY STEPS

1. Baste five small baby-size quilts. Use a panel or 1½ yards of a baby fabric and add two borders: a narrow inner border and a wider outer one. This will give you quilt tops to practice on that don't require a lot of time or work to assemble. Choose a panel or fabric that will keep your interest and give you motifs or designs to follow. Number your quilts 1 through 5.

2. Over the next two weeks, quilt all five quilts, in order from 1 through 5. Make a promise to yourself to quilt every day, even if it's for only 10 minutes. The repetition over the two weeks is very important.

See Pat demonstrate free-motion quilting around shapes at ShopMartingale.com/PatSloanVideos

3. **Write on a piece of paper** the day you started to quilt each quilt, starting with quilt 1. When you finish it, record the date and pin the paper to quilt 1. Do the same for each of the five quilts. When you've finished the first one, start on the next one. Don't stop to attach the binding until all five quilts are done.

4. **When quilt 5 is complete,** get out all five quilts and compare your work. You'll see a huge improvement from quilt 1 to quilt 5.

5. **Now, attach an easy binding** on each quilt. Throw the quilts in the wash and then give them away! I'm serious. Do *not* keep them, because you'll constantly compare what you did. Don't dwell on where you started. You want that feeling of accomplishment, so you can move onto quilt 6!

ALWAYS WARM UP

Anytime you leave large gaps of time between free-motion quilting sessions, you'll need to do a little practice piece to warm up and refresh your muscle memory. Think of it like stretching before an exercise class. Keep a stack of sample quilt sandwiches to stitch on. When they're filled up with quilting, zigzag the edges and use them as dust rags! See, I told you that you'll use *all* the samples *and* real projects. Even a dust rag is useful.

YOU'RE READY FOR A REAL QUILT

Let me tell you a story. I can clearly remember the first quilt I knew I'd gotten right. It was an Ocean Waves design, wall-hanging size, and when I had finished it I was so happy! I remember thinking I liked the quilting, and I was even willing to hang it in a local quilt shop. I loved my work on it and knew that I'd gotten over that learning curve. This feeling of accomplishment will happen to you, too, but you have to do the work by putting in the effort and time to quilt and get better. I know you can do it.

Walking-Foot Quilts

*Now we get to the good part—making quilts! I quilted
the projects in this section using a walking foot.*

Strippy Table Runner

I love learning new things by trying them out on small projects I can sew quickly. Using precut strips in a table runner that's easy to machine quilt lets me try all kinds of different quilting styles on a single project. The strips of this runner give me a place to focus the quilting—I can sew along the lines or across the lines, using them as a guide.

- - - - - - - - - - - - - - - -

Finished runner: 16½" x 36½"

> Sometimes it's the same moments that take your breath away that breathe purpose and love back into your life.
>
> — STEVE MARABOLI —

Materials

Yardage is based on 42"-wide fabric.

2 strips, 2½" x 42", *each* of 3 assorted light and 3 assorted dark prints for runner
¼ yard of dark print for binding
¾ yard of fabric for backing
21" x 40" piece of batting
Freezer paper to mark rounded corners (optional)

Cutting

From *each* of the assorted light and dark strips, cut:
2 strips, 2½" x 17" (24 total)

From the dark print for binding, cut:
2¼"-wide bias strips (enough to yield 120")

Making the Runner

1 Sew nine light and nine dark 2½"-wide strips together along their long edges, alternating the light and dark strips as shown. Press the seam allowances in one direction. (You'll have three light and three dark strips left over for another project.)

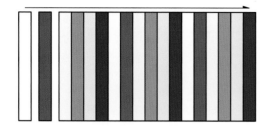

Prevent Bowing

Bowing is a common problem when joining strips along their long edges. Reversing the sewing direction from one seam to the next will help prevent bowing. It's also helpful to carefully pin the strips together, making sure to match the ends and centers of the strips.

2 You can leave the table runner square, or round the corners as I did. To round a corner, trace the quarter-circle pattern at right onto the uncoated side of a piece of freezer paper and cut out the circle. Lightly press the shiny side of the circle on the corner and carefully trim the curve.

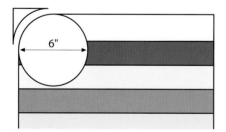

6"

Finishing

For help on binding, download free information at ShopMartingale.com/HowtoQuilt.

1 Referring to "Getting Ready to Machine Quilt" on page 8, layer the runner with batting and backing; baste.

2 Quilt your project. Refer to "Up Close and Beautiful" on page 53 for details on how my runner is quilted.

3 Use the dark 2¼"-wide bias strips to make and attach the binding.

Use a Jelly Roll

I like using a Jelly Roll to make a quick and easy runner. A Jelly Roll is a package of precut 2½"-wide strips from Moda Fabrics. Each Jelly Roll has 40 strips from one fabric line and will make four table runners. To make four runners from one Jelly Roll, cut each strip into two 17"-long pieces. Then separate the strips into four groups of 18 strips each (I used light and dark strips). You'll have eight strips left over for another project.

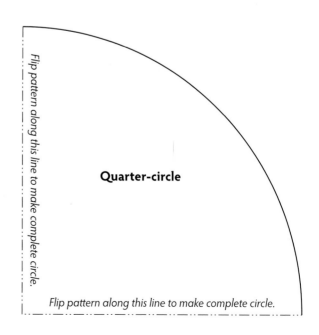

Flip pattern along this line to make complete circle.

Quarter-circle

Flip pattern along this line to make complete circle.

Up Close and Beautiful

Table runners are a perfect size for practicing machine quilting. All three of these were quilted using a walking foot. The navy-and-cream version (top) was quilted in the ditch. The pink version (middle) was quilted with a spiral (see page 26 for more on spirals), and the aqua version (bottom) was quilted with a variety of decorative stitches, each stitched along the center of a fabric strip.

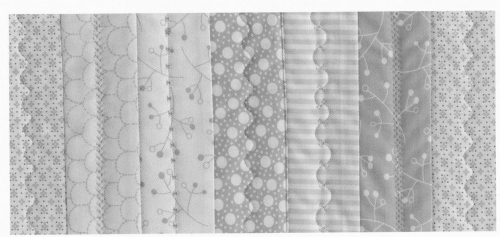

Mini Charm Star

*I love 2½" squares—they're so adorable—*and I love using a full line of Moda mini charm packs! This little star quilt can be used as a wall hanging or table mat. Make it in holiday prints to change your decorations or make several for a larger quilt. The design is also a super way to use up fabric scraps. I cut my scraps into 2½" squares and store them by color, which makes them very easy to work with!

Finished size: 28½" x 28½"

Every accomplishment starts with the decision to try.

— GAIL DEVERS —

Materials

Yardage is based on 42"-wide fabric.

¾ yard of tan print for background for Star block and border

⅓ yard of red print for binding

60 squares, 2½" x 2½", of assorted red, cream, and tan prints for Star block*

12 squares, 2⅞" x 2⅞", of assorted red prints for Star block

1 yard of fabric for backing

32" x 32" piece of batting

A mini charm pack contains 40 squares, 2½" x 2½". If you use 2 mini charm packs, you'll have 20 squares left over for another project. Or, you can use 1 mini charm pack and cut an additional 20 squares from your stash.

Cutting

From the tan print for background, cut:

4 squares, 6⅞" x 6⅞"; cut in half diagonally to yield 8 triangles

4 squares, 6½" x 6½"

2 strips, 2½" x 28½"

2 strips, 2½" x 24½"

From the red print for binding, cut:

4 strips, 2¼" x 42"

Making the Star Quilt

Mix up the 2½" squares so you have four stacks of nine squares each. Set aside the remaining 24 squares for step 3.

1 Lay out the squares from one stack in a nine-patch arrangement as shown, arranging the squares as desired. Join the squares into rows. Press the seam allowances in opposite directions from row to row. Join the rows to make a nine-patch unit. Press the seam allowances in one direction. Make four units that each measure 6½" square.

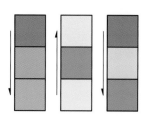

Make 4.

2 Cut the red 2⅞" squares in half diagonally to yield 24 triangles.

3 Lay out three 2½" squares and three triangles from step 2 as shown. Join the triangles and squares into rows. Press the seam allowances as indicated. Join the rows and press. Make eight units.

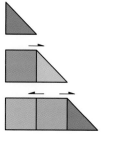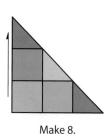

Make 8.

4 Sew a tan triangle to each unit from step 3 to make a star-point unit. Press the seam allowances toward the tan triangle. Make eight star-point units that each measure 6½" square.

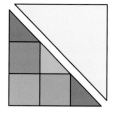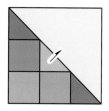

Make 8.

5 Lay out one nine-patch unit, two star-point units, and one tan 6½" square as shown. Join the pieces into rows, and then join the rows to make a quadrant. Press the seam allowances in the directions indicated. Make four quadrants that each measure 12½" square.

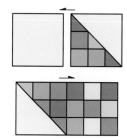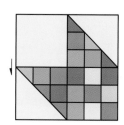

6 Lay out the quadrants as shown in the quilt assembly diagram on page 57, making sure to rotate the quadrants as needed to make a Star block. Join the quadrants into rows, and then join the rows to make a block. Press the seam allowances in the directions indicated. The quilt top should measure 24½" square.

7 Sew the tan 24½"-long strips to the top and bottom of the star. Press the seam allowances toward the tan strips. Sew the tan 28½"-long strips

to the sides of the star to complete the border. Press the seam allowances toward the tan strips.

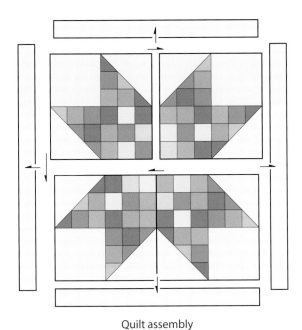

Quilt assembly

Finishing

For help on binding, download free information at ShopMartingale.com/HowtoQuilt.

1 Referring to "Getting Ready to Machine Quilt" on page 8, layer the quilt with batting and backing; baste.

2 Quilt your project. Refer to "Up Close and Beautiful" below for details on how my quilt is quilted.

3 Use the red 2¼"-wide strips to make and attach the binding.

Up Close and Beautiful

Practice straight-line quilting using a straight or decorative stitch to frame the star (below), or start with a freezer-paper circle (see page 26) to begin spiral quilting for a bull's-eye effect (right).

Checkerboard Hearts

As a little girl, I loved trips into Na-Na's attic and bringing down her very old Chinese Checkers game board. I'm not sure anyone really understood how to play, so we made up our own version! Na-Na was a great grandma for a little girl. She got on the floor and played games, and she was fun. She was also the person who noticed that I liked to "make things." These hearts are for you, Na-Na!

- - - - - - - - - - - - - - -

Finished size: 47½" x 47½"
Finished block: 6" x 6"

Nothing is impossible, the word itself says 'I'm possible'!

— AUDREY HEPBURN —

Materials

Yardage is based on 42"-wide fabric.

⅝ yard of cream print for heart blocks and border #2

29 strips, 2½" x 42", of assorted black, red, dark-gray, medium-gray, and cream prints for borders*

2 squares, 5" x 5", *each* of 9 assorted red prints for heart blocks**

4 squares, 5" x 5", of assorted cream prints for corner squares

½ yard of black print for binding

3 yards of fabric for backing

52" x 52" piece of batting

You'll need 3 sets of 2 matching dark-gray strips for border #3.

**You'll need 2 matching squares of each red print.*

Cutting

From *each pair* of red squares, cut:

1 square, 4¼" x 4¼" (9 total); cut the square into quarters diagonally to yield 4 triangles (36 total; 2 will be extra)

1 square, 4" x 4" (9 total)

Continued on page 60

Continued from page 58

From the cream print, cut:

1 strip, 4¼" x 42"; crosscut into 5 squares,
  4¼" x 4¼". Cut the squares into quarters
  diagonally to yield 20 triangles (2 will be extra).
2 strips, 4" x 42"; crosscut into 18 squares, 4" x 4".
  Cut *9 of the squares* in half diagonally to yield 18
  triangles.
2 strips, 1½" x 22½"
2 strips, 1½" x 20½"

From 1 medium-gray 2½"-wide strip, cut:

2 strips, 1½" x 18½"

From 1 medium-gray 2½"-wide strip, cut:

2 strips, 1½" x 20½"

From the remaining 2½"-wide strips, cut a *total* of:

76 rectangles, 2½" x 5"
168 squares, 2½" x 2½"

From *each pair* of dark-gray 2½"-wide strips, cut:

2 strips, 2½" x 13½" (6 total)
2 strips, 2½" x 12" (6 total)

From the black print, cut:

5 strips, 2¼" x 42"

Making the Quilt Center

1 Sew one red and one cream 4¼" triangle
together as shown. Press the seam allowances
toward the red triangle. Make two matching units.
Repeat to make nine pairs of matching units.

Make 2 matching
units (18 total).

2 Sew one cream 4" triangle to one unit from
step 1 as shown. Press the seam allowances
toward the large cream triangle. Make two matching
units. Repeat to make nine pairs of matching units
that measure 3½" square.

Make 2 matching
units (18 total).

3 Draw a diagonal line from corner to corner
on the wrong side of each remaining cream
4" square. Layer a marked square and a red 4"
square, right sides together. Sew a scant ¼" from
each side of the drawn line. Cut the squares apart
on the marked line to make two identical half-
square-triangle units. Press the seam allowances
toward the red triangle. Trim the units to measure
3½" square. Make a total of 18 units.

Make 18.

4 Lay out two units *each* from steps 2 and 3,
all matching, as shown. Join the units into
rows. Press the seam allowances in opposite
directions from row to row. Join the rows and press
the seam allowances in one direction. Make nine
Heart blocks that measure 6½" square.

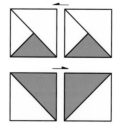 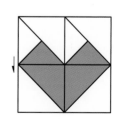

Make 9.

5 Lay out the Heart blocks in three rows of three blocks each. Join the blocks into rows. Press the seam allowances in opposite directions from row to row. Join the rows and press the seam allowances in one direction. The quilt center should measure 18½" square.

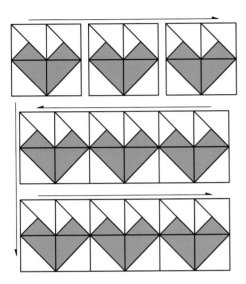

6 Sew the medium-gray 18½"-long strips to the top and bottom of the quilt center. Sew the medium-gray 20½"-long strips to the sides of the quilt center. Press all seam allowances toward the newly added strips.

7 Sew the cream 20½"-long strips to the top and bottom of the quilt center. Sew the cream 22½"-long strips to the sides of the quilt center. Press all the seam allowances toward the newly added strips. The quilt top should now measure 22½" square.

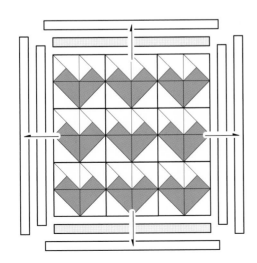

Making the Checkerboard Border

1 Lay out three rows of 11 assorted 2½" squares each, mixing up the squares as shown in the photo on page 58. Join the squares into rows. Press the seam allowances in opposite directions from row to row. Join the rows to make the top border. Press the seam allowances in one direction. Repeat to make the bottom border. These borders should be 22½" long.

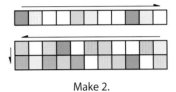

Make 2.

2 Lay out three rows of 17 assorted 2½" squares each, mixing up the squares as shown in the photo. Join the squares into rows. Press the seam allowances in opposite directions from row to row. Join the rows to make a side border. Press the seam allowances in one direction. Repeat to make a second side border. These borders should measure 34½" long.

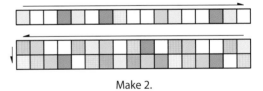

Make 2.

Making the Piano Key Border

1 Sew 19 assorted 2½" x 5" rectangles together side by side in random order to make the top border. Press the seam allowances in one direction. Repeat to make a total of four borders. These borders should be 38½" long.

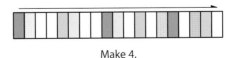

Make 4.

2
Add a cream 5" square to each end of two of the border strips from step 1 to make the side borders. Press the seam allowances as indicated.

Make 2.

Assembling the Quilt Top

1
Sew the top and bottom checkerboard borders to the quilt center. Press the seam allowances toward the quilt center. Sew the side checkerboard borders to the sides of the quilt center. Press the seam allowances toward the quilt center.

2
To make the top-border strip, join three different dark-gray 2½" x 12" strips end to end. Press the seam allowances open to reduce bulk. Trim the strip to measure 34½" long. Repeat to make the bottom-border strip, placing the same dark-gray strip in the center as you did for the top border.

3
To make a side-border strip, join three different dark-gray 2½" x 13½" strips end to end, making sure to place the same dark-gray strip in the center as you did for the top and bottom borders. Press the seam allowances open to reduce bulk. Trim the strip to measure 38½" long. Repeat to make a second side-border strip.

4
Refer to the photo on page 58 for placement guidance. Sew the dark-gray 34½"-long strips to the top and bottom of the quilt top. Sew the dark-gray 38½"-long strips to the sides of the quilt center. Press all seam allowances toward the dark-gray strips.

5
Sew the top and bottom piano key borders to the quilt top. Press the seam allowances toward the dark-gray strips. Sew the side piano key borders to the sides of the quilt center. Press all seam allowances toward the dark-gray strips.

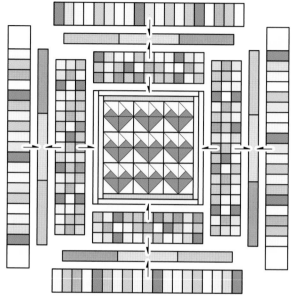

Quilt assembly

Finishing

For help on binding, download free information at ShopMartingale.com/HowtoQuilt.

1
Referring to "Getting Ready to Machine Quilt" on page 8, layer the quilt with batting and backing; baste.

2
Quilt your project. Refer to "Up Close and Beautiful" on page 63 for details on how my quilt is quilted.

3
Use the black 2¼"-wide strips to make and attach the binding.

Up Close and Beautiful

I used my walking foot to quilt a variety of straight-line designs in this quilt. First, I echoed the heart shapes in the quilt center (above). In the checkerboard border, I quilted an X through each square (below). To quilt an X, simply sew diagonally from corner to corner through three squares; when you reach the edge of that border, turn and quilt diagonally in the next group until you make your way around the quilt. In the dark-gray borders, I quilted a long pair of parallel lines running the length of each border.

My Little Kitty

My youngest brother and I share a love of animals.
His childhood pet was a very loving cat named Smokey. Since
I had dogs, cats were a bit of a mystery to me until Smokey joined
our family—although I'm told that Smokey did act a bit more like
a dog than a cat, which might be why I loved him so!

I can see this sweet kitty-appliqué block done in a repeat for
a cozy lap-sized quilt.

Finished Size: 12½" x 15½"

A year from now you may wish you had started today.

— KAREN LAMB —

Materials

Yardage is based on 42"-wide fabric.

½ yard of gray floral for outer border and backing

¼ yard of dark-gray print for inner border and
binding

7½" x 10½" rectangle of cream dot for background

7" x 10" rectangle of medium-gray solid for
kitty appliqué

16" x 19" piece of batting

7" x 10" rectangle of 16"-wide lightweight paper-
backed fusible web

Cutting

From the dark-gray print, cut:
2 strips, 2¼" x 42"
2 pieces, 1" x 11½"
2 pieces, 1" x 7½"

From the gray floral, cut:
1 piece, 16" x 19"*
2 pieces, 2½" x 15½"
2 pieces, 2½" x 8½"

Set aside for backing.

Making the Quilt

1 Trace the kitty pattern on page 67 onto the fusible web. Roughly cut out the shape, about ½" beyond the drawn line. To make the appliqué soft, cut through the excess web around the kitty, through the marked line, and into the interior of the shape. Cut away the excess fusible web on the inside of the kitty, leaving less than ¼" *inside* the drawn line.

Fusible Appliqué

Learn more about my fusible-appliqué techniques in my book Pat Sloan's Teach Me to Appliqué (Martingale, 2015).

2 Position the fusible-web kitty on the medium-gray rectangle. Fuse as instructed by the manufacturer. Cut out the kitty on the marked line and remove the paper backing.

3 Fold the cream rectangle in half horizontally and vertically; finger-press to establish centering lines. Center the fusible-web kitty on the cream rectangle and fuse in place.

4 Sew the dark-gray 7½"-long pieces to the top and bottom of the cream rectangle. Press the seam allowances toward the dark-gray pieces. Sew the dark-gray 11½"-long pieces to the sides of the cream rectangle to complete the inner border. Press the seam allowances toward the dark-gray pieces.

5 Sew the gray-floral 8½"-long pieces to the top and bottom of the quilt top. Press the seam allowances toward the gray-floral pieces. Sew the

Up Close and Beautiful

Use a walking foot to blanket-stitch to stitch around the appliquéd shape. Then stitch straight lines in the background and border as described on page 28.

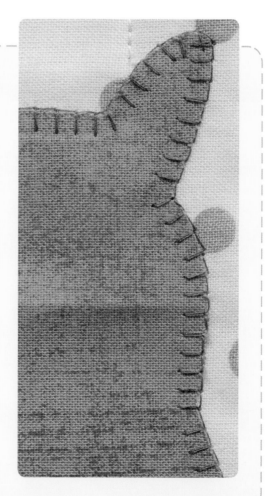

gray-floral 15½"-long pieces to sides of the quilt top to complete the outer border. Press the seam allowances toward the gray-floral pieces.

Pattern does not include seam allowances and is reversed for fusible appliqué.

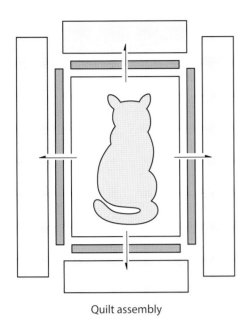

Quilt assembly

Finishing

For help on binding or other finishing techniques, download free information at ShopMartingale.com/HowtoQuilt.

1 Referring to "Getting Ready to Machine Quilt" on page 8, layer the quilt with batting and backing; baste.

2 Quilt your project. Refer to "Up Close and Beautiful" on page 66 for details on how my quilt is quilted.

3 Use the dark-gray 2¼"-wide strips to make and attach the binding.

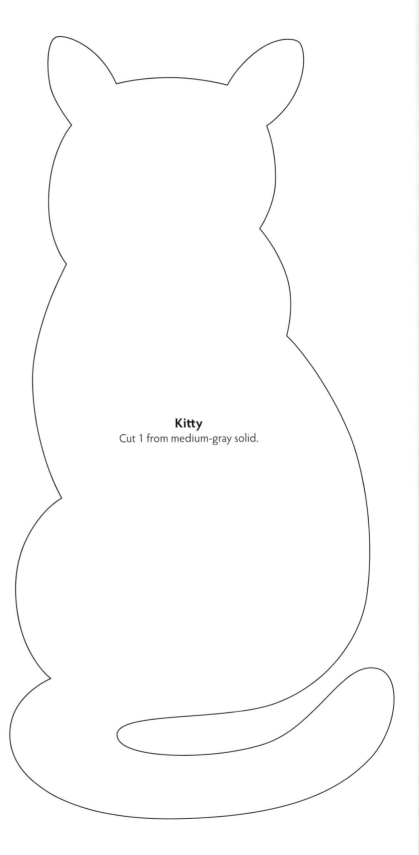

Kitty
Cut 1 from medium-gray solid.

Cherry Pie

Do you have a favorite dessert? Cake, cookies, candy, maybe ice cream? Mine is pie. Cherry pie, to be more specific. Add an amazing crust, and I'll be in heaven. Over the years I've tried my hand at making great piecrust, but I seem to do much better buying an amazing pie and eating it! You might notice I also like red and white. Cherry pie with a scoop of vanilla ice cream fits right in, don't you think?

Finished size: 65½" x 81½"
Finished block: 15" x 15"

There is always something to be grateful for.

— RHONDA BYRNE —

Materials

Yardage is based on 42"-wide fabric.

2⅛ yards of red-and-white floral for blocks and border

1⅞ yards of white solid for blocks and sashing

⅞ yard of red check for blocks, sashing, and binding

⅜ yard of red-and-white dot for blocks

7 fat quarters (18" x 21") of assorted red prints for blocks

9 fat eighths (9" x 21") of assorted white prints for blocks

5 yards of fabric for backing

70" x 86" piece of batting

Cutting

From the white solid, cut:

5 strips, 4" x 42"; crosscut into 48 squares, 4" x 4"

5 strips, 3½" x 42"; crosscut into 48 squares, 3½" x 3½"

14 strips, 1½" x 42"; crosscut *8 of the strips* into:
    10 strips, 1½" x 14½"
    7 strips, 1½" x 13½"
    6 squares, 1½" x 1½"

Continued on page 70

Continued from page 68

From the red check, cut:

8 strips, 2¼" x 42"

4 squares, 4" x 4"

8 squares, 3½" x 3½"

24 squares, 1½" x 1½"

From the red-and-white dot, cut:

8 squares, 4" x 4"

16 squares, 3½" x 3½"

From *each* of 6 assorted red-print fat quarters, cut:

4 squares, 4" x 4" (24 total)

8 squares, 3½" x 3½" (48 total)

From the remaining red-print fat quarter, cut:

4 squares, 4" x 4"

1 rectangle, 3½" x 9½"

10 squares, 3½" x 3½"

From the *lengthwise grain* of the red-and-white floral, cut:

4 strips, 8½" x 65½"

8 squares, 4" x 4"

16 squares, 3½" x 3½"

From *each* of 7 assorted white print fat eighths, cut:

1 rectangle, 3½" x 9½" (7 total)

2 squares, 3½" x 3½" (14 total)

From *each* of 2 assorted white print fat eighths, cut:

2 rectangles, 3½" x 9½" (4 total)

4 squares, 3½" x 3½" (8 total)

Making the Blocks

Instructions are for making one block. For each block, you'll need four red 4" squares and eight red 3½" squares, all matching. You'll also need one white print rectangle and two white print squares, all matching. Note that for one block, as shown in the photo on page 68, you will use a red rectangle and red 3½" squares instead of white pieces for the inner "plus" shape.

1 Draw a diagonal line from corner to corner on the wrong side of each white-solid 4" square. Layer a marked square and a red 4" square, right sides together. Sew a scant ¼" from each side of the drawn line. Cut the squares apart on the marked line to make two identical half-square-triangle units. Trim the units to 3½" x 3½". Press the seam allowances toward the red triangle. Make a total of eight units.

Make 8.

2 Join two half-square-triangle units and one red 3½" square as shown to make a side unit. Press the seam allowances toward the red square. Make four side units. The units should measure 3½" x 9½".

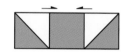

Make 4.

3 Lay out four red 3½" squares, two white print squares, and one white print rectangle as shown. Sew the squares together to make two rows. Press the seam allowances toward the red squares. Sew the rows to the white rectangle to make a center unit. Press the seam allowances toward the red squares. Make one center unit, which should measure 9½" square.

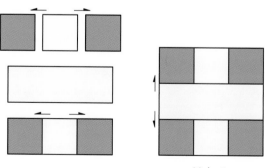

Make 1.

4 Lay out the side units from step 2, four white-solid 3½" squares, and the center unit as shown. Join the pieces into rows. Press the seam allowances as indicated. Join the rows and press the seam allowances toward the center. Repeat the steps to make a total of 12 blocks that measure 15½" square.

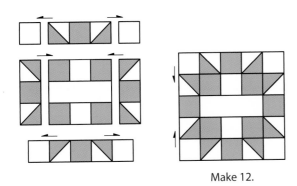

Make 12.

Assembling the Quilt Top

1 To make a side sashing strip, sew a red-check 1½" square to one end of a white-solid 1½" x 14½" strip. Press the seam allowances toward the red square. Make 10 sashing strips that measure 1½" x 15½".

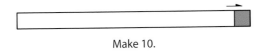

Make 10.

2 To make a center sashing strip, sew red-check 1½" squares to both ends of a white-solid 1½" x 13½" strip. Press the seam allowances toward the red squares. Make seven sashing strips that measure 1½" x 15½".

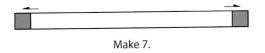

Make 7.

3 Lay out the blocks, sashing strips, and white-solid 1½" squares as shown in the quilt assembly diagram at right. Join the pieces into rows. Press the seam allowances as indicated. Join the rows and press the seam allowances toward the sashing strips.

4 Join the remaining six white-solid 1½"-wide strips end to end. From the pieced strip, cut two 63½"-long strips and two 49½"-long strips. Sew the 63½"-long strips to the sides of the quilt top. Sew the 49½"-long strips to the top and bottom of the quilt top. Press all seam allowances toward the newly added strips.

5 Sew red-and-white floral strips to the sides of the quilt top. Sew red-and-white floral strips to the top and bottom of the quilt top. Press all seam allowances toward the newly added strips.

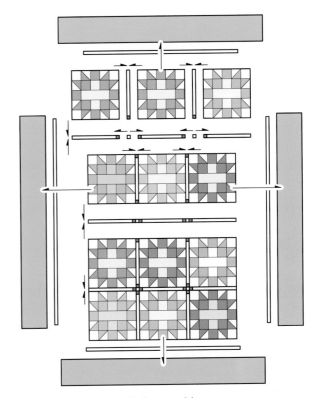

Quilt assembly

Finishing

For help on binding, download free information at ShopMartingale.com/HowtoQuilt.

1 Referring to "Getting Ready to Machine Quilt" on page 8, layer the quilt with batting and backing; baste.

2 Quilt your project. Refer to "Up Close and Beautiful" on page 72 for details on how my quilt is quilted.

3 Use the red-check 2¼"-wide strips to make and attach the binding.

Up Close and Beautiful

This quilt actually features a combination of walking-foot and free-motion quilting. To secure the quilt top, I quilted the wave stitch in all of the sashing pieces using a walking foot. This anchored the quilt top so I could then proceed to stitch a variety of designs in the blocks. Clockwise from top left, I stitched meandering, loops, pebbles or bubbles, and echoes in the block backgrounds. In each plus sign, I simply quilted horizontal rows, back and forth, rounding the curves when I switched directions.

Free-Motion Quilts

When I finally mastered free-motion quilting, I felt like the entire world had opened up. It was easier to maneuver the quilt. I could quilt curves, loops, and swirls. And it gave me the techniques to quilt appliqué pieces effectively! The Strippy Table Runner (page 50) is perfect for practicing.

Blue Lagoon

I took a classic Rail Fence block and added a few more strips than usual. I love the impact of those additional strips, and it's a fun way to use up scrap fabrics! I used the border fabric to select two colors in a variety of prints for the blocks. Quilting allover swirls in block formation gives you a lot of space to practice not only swirls but also how to handle a lap-sized quilt.

- - - - - - - - - - - - - - - - - - - -

Finished size: 64½" x 72½"
Finished block: 8" x 8"

No one can fail if he does his best.

— OSCAR A. KIRKHAM —

Materials

Yardage is based on 42"-wide fabric.

3¾ yards of white-and-blue floral for blocks, inner border, and outer border*
1⅓ yards of blue print for blocks, middle border, and binding (blue #1)
⅝ yard of blue print for blocks (blue #2)
½ yard of blue print for blocks (blue #3)
½ yard *each* of 2 white prints for blocks (white #1 and white #2)
4¼ yards of fabric for backing
72" x 80" piece of batting

If the border fabric is directional and you want all the motifs to go in the same direction, you'll need 1 additional yard of fabric.

Cutting

From the *lengthwise grain* of the white-and-blue floral, cut:
2 strips, 10" x 72½"*
2 strips, 10" x 45½"*
2 strips, 1½" x 50½"
10 strips, 1½" x 50"; crosscut into 49 pieces, 1½" x 8½"
2 strips, 1½" x 40½"

Continued on page 76

Continued on page 76

Continued from page 74

From blue #1, cut:

5 strips, 2" x 42"

8 strips, 2¼" x 42"

9 strips, 1½" x 42"; crosscut into 36 pieces, 1½" x 8½"

From blue #2, cut:

11 strips, 1½" x 42"; crosscut into 44 pieces, 1½" x 8½"

From blue #3, cut:

10 strips, 1½" x 42"; crosscut into 40 pieces, 1½" x 8½"

From white #1, cut:

10 strips, 1½" x 42"; crosscut into 38 pieces, 1½" x 8½"

From white #2, cut:

9 strips, 1½" x 42"; crosscut into 33 pieces, 1½" x 8½"

For directional fabrics, see "Directional Border Fabrics" below.

Directional Border Fabrics

Using a directional fabric *for the outer border requires you to plan ahead. If you want to repeat the motifs in all the borders, be sure to measure the sides of the quilt top before cutting the strips. Then cut the strips as follows:*

- *From the lengthwise grain (parallel to the selvage), cut two strips, 10" x 73½".*

- *From the crosswise grain (across the width of the fabric), cut two strips, 10" x 42". You'll need to cut two strips, 10" x 20", from the crosswise grain. Sew a 20"-long strip to one end of each 42"-long strip, matching the repeats. Then trim each pieced strip to make two strips, 10" x 45½".*

Making the Rail Fence Blocks

Join four blue and four white pieces along their long edges, alternating them as shown to make a block. Note that you'll repeat one blue and one white print in each block. Press the seam allowances toward the blue pieces. The block should measure 8½" square. Make a total of 30 blocks.

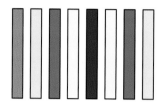 

Make 30.

Assembling the Quilt Top

1 Lay out the blocks in six rows of five blocks each, rotating every other block in each row and from row to row as shown in the quilt assembly diagram on page 77. Sew the blocks together into rows. Press the seam allowances as indicated. Join the rows and press the seam allowances in one direction.

2 Sew the white-and-blue 40½"-long strips to the top and bottom of the quilt center. Sew the white-and-blue 50½"-long strips to the sides of the quilt top. Press all seam allowances toward the white-and-blue strips.

3 Join the blue 2"-wide strips end to end. From the pieced strip, cut two 42½"-long strips and two 53½"-long strips. Sew the 42½"-long strips to the top and bottom of the quilt top. Sew the 53½"-long strips to the sides of the quilt top. Press all seam allowances toward the blue strips.

4 Sew the white-and-blue 45½"-long strips to the top and bottom of the quilt top. Sew the white-and-blue 72½"-long strips to the sides of the quilt top. Press all seam allowances toward the white-and-blue strips.

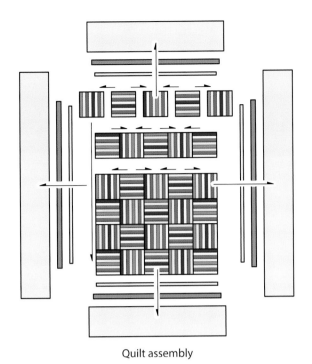

Quilt assembly

Finishing

For help on binding, download free information at ShopMartingale.com/HowtoQuilt.

1 Referring to "Getting Ready to Machine Quilt" on page 8, layer the quilt with batting and backing; baste.

2 Quilt your project. Refer to "Up Close and Beautiful" below for details on how my quilt is quilted.

3 Use the blue 2¼"-wide strips to make and attach the binding.

Up Close and Beautiful

Swirl quilting creates the perfect counterpoint to all the straight lines in this quilt. I simply used the direction of the patchwork blocks as a guide for my swirls. I stitched swirls across one pair of strips, and then switched directions to quilt more swirls on the way back—all without turning the quilt.

Winter Bliss

If you want to stretch your Christmas decorating into winter, use snowmen! I collect snowmen and I'm quite particular about their look. I'm drawn to a certain folk-art style and love snowmen with birds or garden tools or scarves and mittens. Including other elements with your snowman, just as I did in this quilt, is fun. Sprinkle snowmen around the house with your holiday decorations. After Christmas, take down the holiday projects and you're left with snowmen to keep you smiling all winter!

- - - - - - - - - - - - - - - - -

Finished size: 24½" x 28½"

The starting point of all achievement is desire.

— NAPOLEON HILL —

Materials

Yardage is based on 42"-wide fabric unless otherwise noted.

⅝ yard of navy print for outer border and binding

1 fat quarter (18" x 21") of blue print for background

⅓ yard of red print for inner border and corner triangles (red #1)

4" x 5" rectangle of red print for bird (red #2)

6" x 9" rectangle of red print for berries (red #3)

8" x 10" rectangle of cream print for snowman's head and flower petals (cream #1)

6" x 6" square of cream print for snowman's middle (cream #2)

9" x 10" rectangle of cream print for snowman's bottom (cream #3)

6" x 10" rectangle of cream print for flower petals (cream #4)

7" x 7" square of black print for bird's wing and snowman's hat and arms

8" x 10" rectangle of green print for holly leaves (green #1)

8" x 10" rectangle of green print for holly leaves (green #2)

8" x 10" square of green print for stems (green #3)

1" x 2" rectangle of orange print for snowman's nose

1 yard of fabric for backing

Continued on page 80

Continued from page 78

28" x 32" piece of batting

1⅛ yards of 16"-wide lightweight paper-backed fusible web

2 black buttons, ½" diameter, for snowman's eyes

½" bias-tape maker

Appliqué basting glue

Cutting

From red #1, cut:

2 strips, 1½" x 42"; crosscut into:

    2 strips, 1½" x 18½"

    2 strips, 1½" x 16½"

2 squares, 5" x 5"

From the navy print, cut:

2 strips, 4½" x 42"; crosscut into:

    2 strips, 4½" x 20½"

    2 strips, 4½" x 16½"

3 strips, 2¼" x 42"

2 squares, 5" x 5"

From the blue print, cut:

1 rectangle, 14½" x 18½"

From green #3, cut:

6 strips, 1" x 10"

Making the Quilt Top

1 Draw a diagonal line from corner to corner on the wrong side of each red #1 square. Layer a marked square and a navy square, right sides together. Sew a scant ¼" from each side of the drawn line. Cut the squares apart on the marked line to make two identical half-square-triangle units. Press the seam allowances toward the navy triangle. Trim the units to measure 4½" x 4½". Make a total of four units.

4½"

4½"

Make 4.

2 Sew red 18½"-long strips to the sides of the blue rectangle. Press the seam allowances toward the red strips. Sew red 16½"-long strips to the top and bottom of the blue rectangle. Press the seam allowances toward the red strips.

3 Sew navy 20½"-long strips to the sides of the quilt top. Press the seam allowances toward the navy strips.

4 Sew half-square-triangle units to both ends of a navy 16½"-long strip as shown in the quilt assembly diagram below. Make two strips and sew them to the top and bottom of the quilt top. Press the seam allowances toward the navy strips.

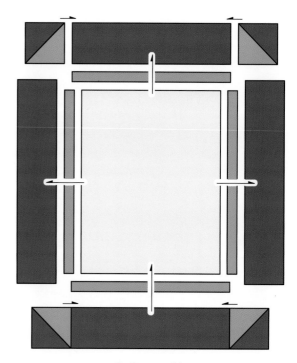

Quilt assembly

Adding the Appliqués

You can find more about my fusible-appliqué techniques in my book *Pat Sloan's Teach Me to Appliqué* (Martingale, 2015).

1 Using the patterns on pages 82–84, trace the number of shapes indicated on the patterns onto the fusible web. Roughly cut out each shape, about ½" beyond the drawn line. On the larger shapes, such as the snowman's head, cut through the excess web around the shape, through the marked line, and into the interior of the shape. Then cut away the excess fusible web on the *inside* of the shape, leaving less than ¼" inside the drawn line.

2. Position the fusible-web shapes on the fabrics indicated on the patterns. Fuse as instructed by the manufacturer. Cut out the shapes on the marked line and remove the paper backing from each shape.

3. Fold the quilt top in half horizontally and vertically; finger-press to establish centering lines. Referring to the photo on page 78, position the prepared appliqué shapes on the quilt top in the following order: Center the flower petals and red dot at the bottom of the quilt top, on top of the borders. Position the snowman, and then add his nose, arms, and hat. Add the bird and its wing. Place three holly leaves and a berry on each side of the snowman. Position one holly leaf and two berries on each side of the flower.

4. For the stems, place one end of a green #3 strip into a ½" bias-tape maker. Pull just the tip of the strip through the bias-tape maker and pin it to your ironing board. Continue to pull the bias-tape maker slowly along the strip, following close behind it with your iron to crease the edges of the fabric as it emerges from the bias-tape maker. Make six stems.

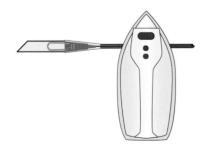

Basting Glue

I use basting glue to draw my stem line and then position the stem on top of the line of glue.

5. Tucking the end of the stems under the flower petals, holly leaves, and/or berries, position the stems on the quilt top. Trim the stems as needed.

6. Fuse the appliqués in place. Blanket-stitch around the outer edge of each shape using a matching or slightly contrasting thread. For the arms and nose, zigzag stitch down the center of the shape using a matching thread color.

Finishing

For help on binding, download free information at ShopMartingale.com/HowtoQuilt.

1. Referring to "Getting Ready to Machine Quilt" on page 8, layer the quilt with batting and backing; baste.

2. Quilt your project. Refer to "Up Close and Beautiful" on page 82 for details on how my quilt is quilted.

3. Use the navy 2¼"-wide strips to make and attach the binding. Add the black buttons for the snowman's eyes as shown in the photo on page 79.

Up Close and Beautiful

Nothing says "swirls" like a snowstorm, so I quilted blue swirls on both the background and Mr. Snowman. I added dimension to the holly leaves by quilting veins in them.

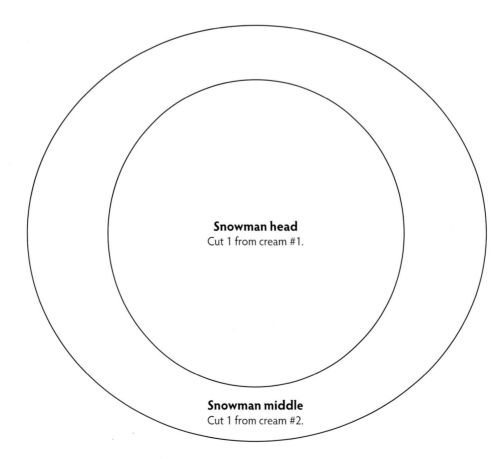

Snowman head
Cut 1 from cream #1.

Snowman middle
Cut 1 from cream #2.

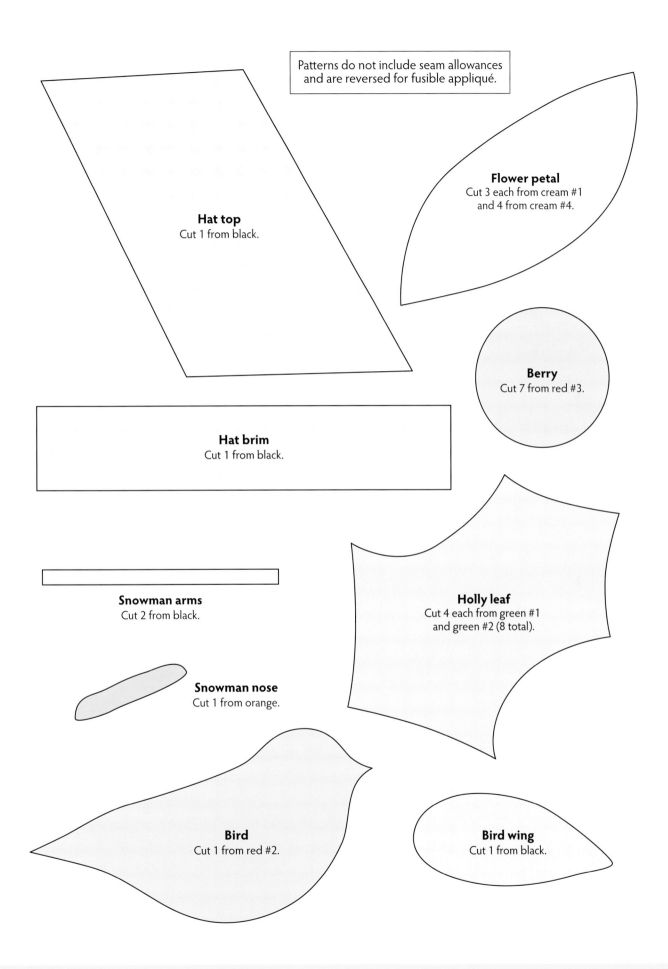

Patterns do not include seam allowances and are reversed for fusible appliqué.

Hat top
Cut 1 from black.

Flower petal
Cut 3 each from cream #1 and 4 from cream #4.

Berry
Cut 7 from red #3.

Hat brim
Cut 1 from black.

Snowman arms
Cut 2 from black.

Holly leaf
Cut 4 each from green #1 and green #2 (8 total).

Snowman nose
Cut 1 from orange.

Bird
Cut 1 from red #2.

Bird wing
Cut 1 from black.

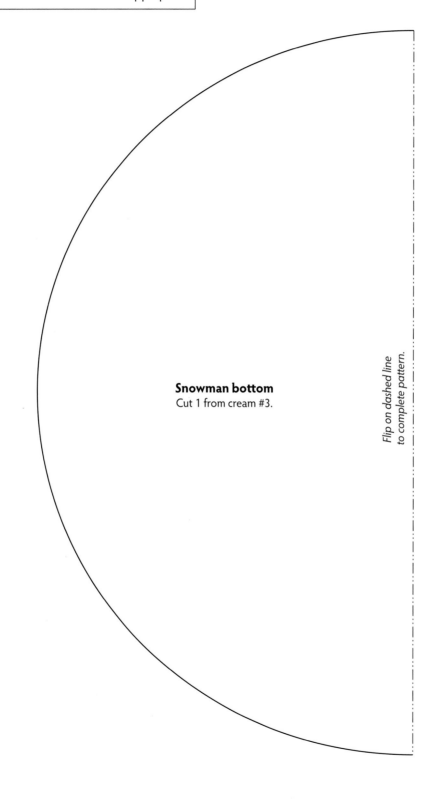

Pattern does not include seam allowances
and is reversed for fusible appliqué.

Snowman bottom
Cut 1 from cream #3.

*Flip on dashed line
to complete pattern.*

Dresden Candy Dish

Dresden plates create such a classic quilt block.

I've been in love with them in every variation I see. When the Moda mini charm packs were developed, my fingers started itching to stitch up something a bit different with them. What if I sewed a few together and then cut out a Dresden blade? When the block was done, it reminded me of one of my Granny's candy dishes, filled with colorful wrapped goodies!

- - - - - - - - - - - - - - - -

Finished size: 15½" x 15½"

Materials

Yardage is based on 42"-wide fabric.

40 squares, 2½" x 2½", of assorted prints for Dresden blades*
1 fat quarter (18" x 21") of white solid for background
¼ yard of red print for binding
1 fat quarter of fabric for backing
18" x 18" piece of batting
Template plastic or EZ Dresden ruler
Glue stick

You can make this project with one Moda mini charm pack of 40 squares, 2½" x 2½".

Cutting

From the white solid, cut:
1 square, 15½" x 15½"

From the red print, cut:
2 strips, 2¼" x 42"

It isn't what we say
or think that defines us,
but what we do.

— JANE AUSTEN —

Making the Dresden Plate

1 Join two print squares to make a two-patch unit. Press the seam allowances in one direction. Make 20 units.

Make 20.

2 (Skip this step if you're using a Dresden ruler.) Trace the wedge pattern on page 89 onto template plastic, making sure to include the centerline. Cut out the wedge template, cutting directly on the line.

3 Place the wedge template on top of a two-patch unit, aligning the wider end of the template with a short, raw edge of the unit as shown. The centerline on the template should be aligned with the seamline. Carefully cut along both long edges of the template to make a wedge. Make 20 wedges.

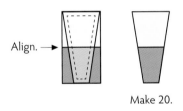

Align. →

Make 20.

4 Fold a wedge in half lengthwise, right sides together, and sew across the wider end using a ¼" seam allowance. You can chain piece these seams to speed up the process. Trim a tiny triangle from the folded seam allowance as shown. Turn the piece right side out and use a bluntly pointed object (such as a knitting needle or chopstick) to push the tip out so it's pointy and the piece is blade shaped. Press the blade flat.

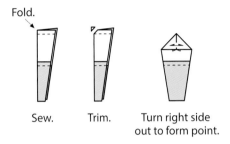

Fold.

Sew.   Trim.   Turn right side out to form point.

5 Repeat with all the pieces to make 20 blades.

Dresden Ruler

If you're using a ruler, align the 4½" line on the ruler with the short, raw edge of the unit as shown. Cut along both long edges of the ruler to make a wedge. Make 20 wedges.

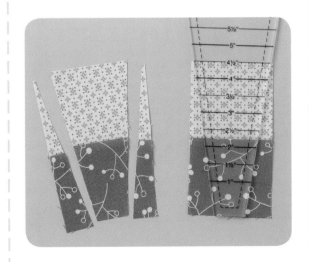

6 Aligning the shoulders of the blades and using a ¼" seam allowance, sew 10 blades together to make a half Dresden plate. Press the seam allowances in one direction. Repeat to make a second half Dresden plate.

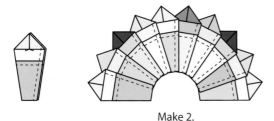

Make 2.

Piecing Tip

When joining the blades, start ½" down from the shoulder and sew two or three stitches. Backstitch to the top edge of the blades and then sew the entire seam. By not starting at the edge of the blade, you'll be sure that the ends of the threads will be hidden.

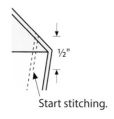

½"

Start stitching.

7 Sew the two halves together to make a ring. Press the seam allowances in one direction.

8 The center of the plate is open. To create a finished edge in the center, roll under a ¼" seam allowance. On the wrong side, use a glue stick to dab a little glue along the edge to hold the seam allowance in place.

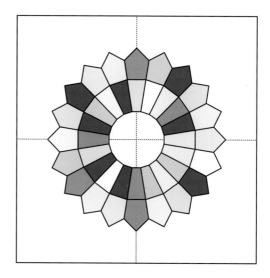

Appliquéing the Dresden Plate

1 Fold the white square in half horizontally and vertically; finger-press to establish centering lines. Unfold and use the creased lines to center the Dresden Plate on the white square. Pin in place.

2 Blanket-stitch around the outer edges and the center of the Dresden Plate.

Finishing

For help on binding, download free information at ShopMartingale.com/HowtoQuilt.

1 Referring to "Getting Ready to Machine Quilt" on page 8, layer the quilt with batting and backing; baste.

2 Quilt your project. Refer to "Up Close and Beautiful" on page 89 for details on how my quilt is quilted.

3 Use the red 2¼"-wide strips to make and attach the binding.

Up Close and Beautiful

To define the shapes, I quilted a free-form spiral in the center of each Dresden plate, and then outlined the blades. Bubbles add a dash of fun to the outer edges of the plates. A long loop was quilted in the center of each blade.

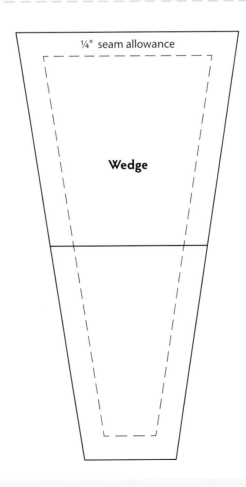

¼" seam allowance

Wedge

Mexican Rose

I'm in love with antique quilts—they inspire me in so many ways. Anytime I can visit my friend Cindy Rennels's booth at a show, I'm thrilled to see what antique quilts she has. One year she had a vintage Mexican Rose quilt. I really loved the block in her quilt. I came right home and sketched a version that was simpler and used modern appliqué techniques. I hope you'll make your own Mexican Rose and send me a photo!

- - - - - - - - - - - - - -

Finished size: 56½" x 56½"
Finished blocks: 19" x 19" and 8" x 8"

Imagination is the eye of the soul.

— JOSEPH JOUBERT —

Materials

Yardage is based on 42"-wide fabric.

1½ yards of white-on-white print for block background
1¼ yards of green print for leaves, stems, inner border, and binding
1⅛ yards of red-and-white floral for outer border
⅝ yard of red print for petals (red #1)
⅜ yard of red print for petals (red #2)
¼ yard of gold print for circles
3¾ yards of fabric for backing
64" x 64" piece of batting
3¼ yards of 16"-wide lightweight paper-backed fusible web

Cutting

From the green print, cut:
4 strips, 1½" x 42"; crosscut into:
   2 strips, 1½" x 38½"
   2 strips, 1½" x 40½"
1 rectangle, 7" x 10"
6 strips, 2¼" x 42"

From the white-on-white print, cut:
4 squares, 19½" x 19½"
4 squares, 8½" x 8½"

From the red-and-white floral, cut:
4 strips, 8½" x 40½"

Making the Appliqué Blocks

You can find out more about my fusible-appliqué techniques in my book *Pat Sloan's Teach Me to Appliqué* (Martingale, 2015).

1 Cut a 6½" x 9½" rectangle of fusible web. Center and fuse the fusible-web rectangle to the wrong side of the green rectangle. Then from the fused rectangle, cut 16 stems, ¼" x 3", for the center blocks and 4 stems, ¼" x 4", for the corner blocks.

2 Using the patterns on page 94, trace onto the fusible web the number of shapes indicated on the patterns. Roughly cut out each shape, about ½" beyond the drawn line. On the larger shapes, such as the circles, cut through the excess web around the shape, through the marked line, and into the interior of the shape. Then cut away the excess fusible web on the *inside* of the shape, leaving less than ¼" inside the drawn line.

3 Position the fusible-web shapes on the fabrics indicated on the patterns. Fuse as instructed by the manufacturer. Cut out the shapes on the marked line and remove the paper backing from each shape.

4 Fold a white 19½" square in half horizontally and vertically; finger-press to establish centering lines. Unfold and refold the white square *diagonally* in both directions; finger-press. Referring to the appliqué placement diagram, position the prepared appliqué shapes on the square in the following order: Place a 3"-long green stem on each horizontal and vertical line. Place a leaf on each diagonal line; notice that one line has two leaves. Arrange three petals and three reversed petals at the top of each stem. Position a small circle at the base of each flower and a large circle in the block

center. Make four center blocks. You'll have one large circle left over to use when assembling the quilt top.

Appliqué placement

5 Fold a white 8½" square in half diagonally. Position the prepared appliqué shapes on the square in the following order: Position a 4"-long green stem on the diagonal line. Arrange three petals and three reversed petals at the top of the stem. Position a small circle at the base of the flower. Make four corner blocks.

6 Fuse the appliqués in place. Blanket-stitch around the outer edge of each shape using a matching or slightly contrasting thread.

Assembling the Quilt Top

1 Lay out the center blocks in two rows of two blocks each, rotating the blocks so the leaves meet in the center as shown in the quilt assembly diagram on page 93. Join the blocks into rows. Press the seam allowances in opposite directions from row to row. Join the rows and press the seam allowances in one direction.

2 Fuse the remaining large gold circle in the center of the quilt top. Blanket-stitch around the circle.

3 Sew the green 38½"-long strips to the top and bottom of the quilt top. Press the seam allowances toward the green strips. Sew the green 40½"-long strips to the sides of the quilt top. Press the seam allowances toward the green strips.

4 Sew red-and-white 40½"-long strips to the sides of the quilt top. Press the seam allowances toward the red-and-white strips.

5 Sew appliquéd corner blocks to both ends of a red-and-white 40½"-long strip as shown in the quilt assembly diagram. Press the seam allowances toward the red-and-white strip. Make two strips and sew them to the top and bottom of the quilt top.

Finishing

For help on binding, download free information at ShopMartingale.com/HowtoQuilt.

1 Referring to "Getting Ready to Machine Quilt" on page 8, layer the quilt with batting and backing; baste.

2 Quilt your project. Refer to "Up Close and Beautiful" below for details on how my quilt is quilted.

3 Use the green 2¼"-wide strips to make and attach the binding.

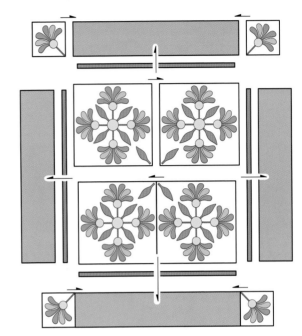

Quilt assembly

Up Close and Beautiful

I started by outline quilting around each appliqué shape using white thread. Then I quilted the entire background with free-motion loops and curls. Inside each yellow dot, I quilted a pretty swirl. I left the rest of the appliqué shapes unquilted. Since the shapes are not too big, it works for this design. I stitched a straight line in the inner border. For the outer border, I again quilted free-motion loops and curls, adding little flower and leaf shapes along the way.

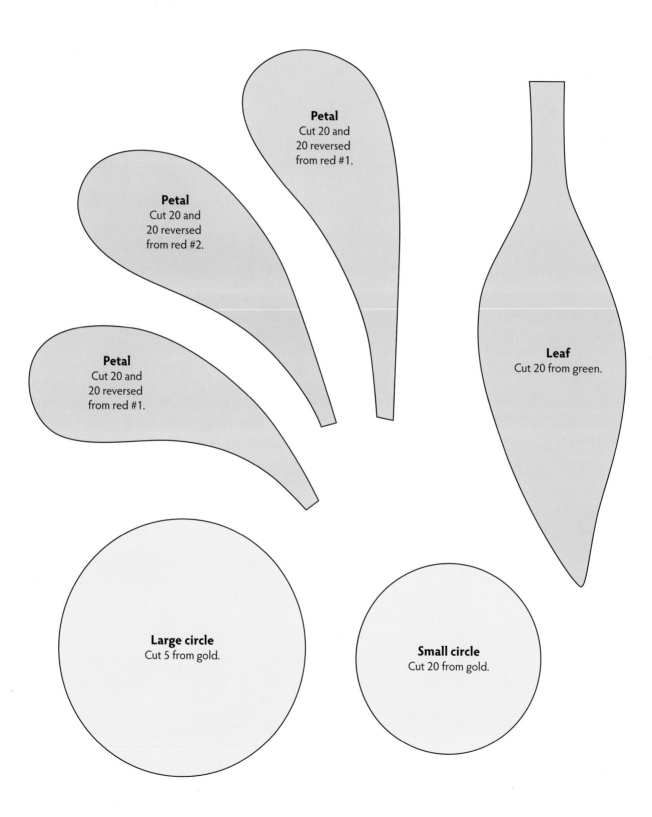

Patterns do not include seam allowances and are reversed for fusible appliqué.

Petal
Cut 20 and 20 reversed from red #1.

Petal
Cut 20 and 20 reversed from red #2.

Petal
Cut 20 and 20 reversed from red #1.

Leaf
Cut 20 from green.

Large circle
Cut 5 from gold.

Small circle
Cut 20 from gold.

Acknowledgments

Many thanks to:

- **Lina LaMora,** who helped me meet stitching deadlines.

I also work with amazing partners in the industry:

- **Moda Fabrics** not only prints my fabric line, but their fabrics in general are the ones I tend to hoard the most. Plus, they shared wonderful props to make this book delightful.

- **Aurifil** creates beautiful-quality thread that I love in a delicious array of colors.

- Thanks to **Tacony Corporation** for the Baby Lock sewing machine I use at home and for the photos in this book.

- **Therm O Web** has the most consistent and dependable fusible web, HeatnBond Lite.

- **Pellon** and **Mountain Mist** battings add the best middle layer to my quilts.

- **Sullivans USA** and **Havel's Sewing** provide me with awesome notions such as rulers and scissors.

- **Reliable** manufactures irons that live up to their name.

- **Olfa** makes the best rotary cutter ever.

Meet Pat

I'm a quilt designer, author, teacher, radio/podcast show producer and host, and fabric designer. My passion for making quilts, sharing quilts, and talking with quilters about quilts is limitless. I travel across the world teaching and host several Internet groups of quilters where we share on a daily basis what we make. And I write about quilting on my blog. To find me, go to PatSloan.com, sign up for my newsletter, and let's chat soon!

Sew
10 minutes
a day.
— PAT SLOAN —